ANTONIO CARLUCCIO
my favourite italian recipes

This paperback edition first published in Australia and New Zealand by
BBC Worldwide Ltd in 2003. Previously published in hardback in 2002.

BBC Worldwide Ltd,
Woodlands, 80 Wood Lane,
London W12 0TT

The recipes contained in this book first appeared in *Antonio Carluccio's Italian Feast*,
which was originally published by BBC Worldwide in 1996 (photographs by Graham
Kirk and Cassie Farrell), and *Antonio Carluccio's Southern Italian Feast*, which was
originally published by BBC Worldwide in 1998 (photographs by Philip Webb and
Steve Watkins).

ISBN 0 563 48725 9

Commissioning Editor: Vivien Bowler
Project Editor: Vicki Vrint
Design Manager: Sarah Ponder
Designer: Kathryn Gammon
Typographic Styling: Paul Welti
Picture Researcher: Claire Parker
Production Controller: Kenneth McKay
Author Photograph: Steve Watkins

Set in HelveticaNeue
Printed and bound in England by Butler and Tanner Ltd, Frome, Somerset
Colour origination by Radstock Reproductions Ltd, Midsomer Norton

*Some of the recipes in this book include wild mushrooms. Cooking and eating some
species of wild mushroom can be dangerous. If you have any doubts at all about the
species of fungus you have picked, do not eat it. Neither the publisher nor the author
can accept any responsibility for the consequences of any mistaken identification of
mushroom species.*

Front cover photograph by Graham Kirk: *Vegetarian Timbale* (page 104)

ANTONIO CARLUCCIO

my favourite italian recipes

contents

introduction

I was delighted to be asked if I would choose my favourite recipes from *Italian Feast* and *Southern Italian Feast* for Australia and New Zealand. It was difficult for me to choose just 100 dishes that represent Italian regional food. Those that I've axed are no less interesting – I have simply selected recipes that are more representative of the cuisine I grew up with and that I love most.

When I was filming my television series throughout Italy, I met so many dedicated and passionate people who had one thing in common – the culture of eating well – although they had no interest in the regional cuisine of their immediate neighbours! This regional culinary patriotism is typical in Italy where the North is oblivious to what the South is producing and vice versa. It is a fact, though, that once Italians sit down for a meal together, all social and political differences disappear as if by magic. They are all interested in enjoying well-prepared, well-cooked food, using local produce of the best quality.

I will never forget the fish market of The Rialto in Venice, which I visited together with Count Carlo Maria Rocca, who has sadly passed away since. His enthusiasm for cooking was well respected by the local fishmongers who were eager to offer him the best of the day's catch. People still tell me today that they cooked the recipes that Carlo presented in the television show. His recipes, which were based on potatoes and monkfish, conjured up the true Italian spirit of cooking to achieve maximum flavour with minimum fuss.

I started to cook in my twenties, as a student in Vienna, at a time of my life when good food was essential. In order to continue enjoying the wonderful dishes I was brought up with, I had to learn to prepare them myself. The time I spent watching my mother cook throughout my childhood left me with only a vague idea of how to complete the dishes on my own, so I was often calling her for culinary advice. I have managed, over the last 40 years, to learn what cooking is all about, and get the most rewarding satisfaction from producing decent, wholesome food for my friends and family.

After many years of wandering through Europe, I arrived in Britain in 1975 and, by pure chance, became a professional cook. Since then I have written many books and made several television programmes, including the two series upon which this book is based.

It would be unfair to say it is easy to prepare good Italian food, as you need a knowledge of Italian flavours that is inherent in our culture and, unless you have lived in Italy for a long time, it is difficult to develop this. But the recipes I have chosen here will show you how to combine these flavours successfully. (Most of the ingredients used are now readily available in good delicatessens and supermarkets.) An entire new culinary world will appear to you, and you should enjoy gratitude and deserved applause from your guests.

Buona Fortuna e Buon Appetito!

Antonio Carluccio

larder

Italian cooking is based on fresh ingredients, so there are not many items you need to keep in stock at home. These are more or less the only ingredients I would suggest you need in your store cupboard.

fats and oils

I use both butter and olive oil on a daily basis. Butter tends to be used more in the north of Italy and is always unsalted. In addition, I suggest you stock at least three different types of oil.

Firstly, a seed oil, like sunflower oil, is good for frying. Secondly, a pure olive oil should be used for the base of sauces and for frying certain foods where you want to retain the sweet taste of olives. Thirdly, you should keep a really good extra virgin olive oil. Italian is best because you can rely on it being really virgin and because of its aroma, typical of the area it comes from. However, good-quality extra virgin olive oil should not be used in cooking as this flavour is lost. This type of oil is ideal eaten raw on salads or as a condiment on warm food.

vinegars

I keep a good *aceto di vino rosso*, Chianti red wine vinegar, for use on salads and in sauces or marinades. Balsamic vinegar is more difficult to choose because the various types vary in quality and so the price ranges from moderate to very expensive. These can be added to sauces, vinaigrettes and extra-fine marinades.

pasta

I suggest that in your store cupboard you always keep a packet of short, dried pasta such as tubettini or farfalline for soups or minestrone, a packet of spaghetti, a packet of larger shaped pasta, such as conchiglie and a packet of egg tagliatelle nests.

polenta

For good polenta, you would use traditional *farina di polenta*: to cook it takes 40 minutes of constant stirring. Nowadays you can buy 'quick' polenta, which is ready in just 5 minutes and offers a good alternative.

pulses and grains

cannellini beans

These are found in any decent larder. Cannellini beans are usually dried but sometimes canned for immediate use.

borlotti beans

Used in the same way as cannellini beans.

broad beans

Very popular fresh in season but in the larder you will find some *fave secche* for winter – dried broad beans which are either turned into soups or are puréed and served with olive oil and wild chicory to make the Pugliese dish *'ncapriata* (see page 115).

chickpeas

Another favourite, they are used mainly for soups and *pasta e ceci*, but also in stews, salads and as an accompaniment to pork dishes.

lentils

Very popular in the south of Italy, they tend to be stewed or made into soups. They are exceptionally good cooked with borage, Campanian-style (see page 20).

rice

Rice is used for stuffing tomatoes and peppers, to make the famous Sicilian *Arancini* (see page 33) and in soups. It can also be eaten plain, with just a little butter or olive oil. The best rice for making the traditional risotto is carnaroli, the Rolls Royce of rice. For Venetian risottos, the best is vialone nano. Arborio rice is also good and remember only these types of rice should be used for risotto.

dried breadcrumbs

Dried breadcrumbs (*pane grattugiato*) are indispensable in the kitchen for dusting meat or vegetables before frying, and may also be added to stuffings or used to thicken sauces.

tomatoes

Absolutely essential in Italian cooking, tomatoes are used daily in one way or another and are preserved in various ways so their flavour can be enjoyed all year round.

pomodori pelati

Peeled tomatoes, traditionally canned or bottled, mostly used in winter when fresh ones are not available. The best are preserved in Salerno, using San Marzano plum tomatoes – excellent for sauces.

polpa di pomodoro

(tomato pulp or crushed tomatoes)
Consists of chunks of deseeded tomatoes in their own juice. It is suitable for any type of sauce.

passata

A smoother version of *polpa*. Both *polpa* and *passata* are beginning to overtake the traditional peeled tomatoes in popularity.

concentrato di pomodoro

(tomato paste)
Available in two forms: as double concentrate and as six-times concentrate, a very dark, thick paste known as *estratto*. Both are used as flavourings and to thicken tomato sauces. I like *estratto* spread on toasted bread, rubbed with garlic and drizzled with olive oil.

pomodori in bottiglia

Made at home by quartering ripe San Marzano plum tomatoes, then pushing them into a bottle. If you make a sauce with these tomatoes, the full summer flavour comes back even in the depths of winter. Or buy in jars from good delicatessans.

pomodori secchi

(sun-dried tomatoes)
Prepared in August and September. Halved tomatoes are sprinkled with coarse salt and laid out on tables under the hot sun to dry. They are later rehydrated with water and vinegar to serve as delicious morsels for the *antipasto* or to flavour soups and sauces.

herbs

The only dried herb I would keep is wild oregano and this is suitable

Baskets of garlic (above) and small snails (below) on a typical market stall.

only for certain sauces and not for everything. Otherwise fresh basil, fresh mint and fresh rosemary are always part of my culinary vocabulary.

salt and pepper

These are culinary essentials. Salt not only brings out the flavour of food but is also used for preserving and as a thick crust in which to bake fish. There are two types of salt, *sale fine* and *sale grosso* (coarse sea salt). Pepper is mostly black and is either freshly ground or added whole to broths and stock. It is also used to make salami.

peperoncini

Peperoncino, or dried chilli, is also called *diavulillo* (little devil) because of its ferociously hot power.

fennel seeds

Fennel seeds are added to various dishes, breads and even sausages for their distinctive flavour.

fresh garlic, onions and shallots

These should always be available. They are an integral part of every sauce and dish, and handy to have in your larder because they keep for quite some time.

capers

These are available both in brine and in vinegar, but I prefer the Sicilian ones from Lipari kept in salt. They have a wonderful flavour – keep two sizes, very small to use whole and large to be chopped.

preserved meat

Below are the main salted and air-dried pork preserves used in Italian cooking.

guanciale

Consists of the cheek of the pig, a fatty, layered cut which is salt-cured and dried. It is used in many sauces, soups and ragùs.

lardo

A thick layer of pork fat, sometimes as much as 10 cm (4 in) deep. It is cut into small cubes and fried with onions and herbs to make a flavoursome base for all sorts of soups, sauces and meat ragùs.

prosciutto crudo

A type of cured ham, it is the hind leg of the pig, which is salted and then air-dried for at least a year. The Southern version is saltier.

cheese

mozzarella

The international demand for mozzarella is so huge that the cows' milk version is now made all over Italy. The very best mozzarella is made with milk from buffaloes. Genuine fresh buffalo mozzarella is wonderful and should be eaten on the day it is made. It is difficult to buy this type of mozzarella outside Italy because of the problem of transporting it. The next best thing is *mozzarella di bufala*, which is sold in a sealed plastic bag containing some of the whey to keep the cheese fresh and moist.

Mozzarella has hundreds of uses in cooking, such as on pizza, in calzone, or sliced and added to vegetable and pasta timbales.

scamorza and provola

Scamorza is sometimes sliced and grilled, while provola can be eaten as a table cheese or used in cooking.

provolone

A huge, cows' milk cheese with a layered structure like mozzarella. It is available as *dolce* (mild) and *piccante* (piquant). Both versions are used as table cheeses and as ingredients in other dishes.

caciocavallo

Similar to provolone but has a stronger flavour and firmer texture. Made of sheep's milk, it is a typical Sicilian cheese. It can be cut into cubes and grilled, added to vegetable stuffings, or grated for use instead of Parmesan.

pecorino

The archetypal sheep's milk cheese. Pecorino is available both fresh and aged. *Caciotta*, the fresh version, is eaten as a table cheese, while *stagionato*, the firmer, aged variety, can be grated as well.

ricotta

A soft, low-fat cheese, it is really a by-product of cheesemaking, since it is made from the whey that has separated from the curd. Ricotta, which has to be eaten very fresh, can be used in hundreds of dishes, both savoury and sweet, and is particularly popular as a filling for calzoni and tarts.

anchovies and tuna

Most Italians keep anchovies in the larder – if not the salted variety, which are the most flavoursome, then at least in oil.

Tuna is canned mostly in oil and is another convenient staple for salads, vegetable stuffings and sauces.

olives

Olives are a precious fruit, essential to all sorts of dishes, and in the land of the olive they are offered to the buyer in an infinite variety of forms. Italians love to eat little snacks or *antipasti* containing black or green olives that have been 'improved' by mixing them with fennel seeds, garlic and chilli or even baking them in the oven, where they become dry and concentrated in flavour. Salads, pasta sauces, stews and roasts often contain olives.

nuts and dried fruit

pine kernels

Small, longish white seeds from the cones of the umbrella pine. They are commonly used in salads, meat and vegetable stuffings, biscuits and cakes.

hazelnuts

Almost exclusively used in biscuits and cakes or eaten like fruit.

almonds

Eaten more than any other nut in the south of Italy. The almond tree, which resembles a peach tree, is cultivated in Puglia, Calabria, Campania, Sardinia and especially in Sicily, where almonds are mostly turned into marzipan to make rich sweets such as *cassata* and various biscuits similar to amaretti.

1

soups & starters

summer bread salad
panzanella marinara

Here is a simple, tasty recipe that includes all the elements of the healthy Mediterranean diet. The ingredients are almost always available in a Southern Italian household and do not cost very much. It is often made with *frisella*, a round or oblong flat loaf that is baked like ordinary bread, then thickly sliced and baked again to dry out so it keeps almost indefinitely, but my mother used leftover bread, dried in the oven the better to absorb the juice of the ripe tomatoes. Ideal as a starter on a summer's day.

SERVES 4

8 SLICES OF WHITE, COUNTRY-STYLE BREAD, DRIED IN A LOW OVEN

300 G (11 OZ) CHERRY TOMATOES, CUT INTO QUARTERS

1 BUNCH OF SPRING ONIONS, FINELY CHOPPED

1 YELLOW PEPPER, CUT INTO SMALL CUBES

1 GARLIC CLOVE, VERY FINELY CHOPPED

20 GREEN OLIVES, PITTED AND HALVED

20 BASIL LEAVES, PLUS SPRIGS TO GARNISH

120 ML (4 FL OZ) VIRGIN OLIVE OIL

1 TABLESPOON STRONG RED WINE VINEGAR

8 ANCHOVY FILLETS, QUARTERED

SALT AND FRESHLY GROUND BLACK PEPPER

METHOD

Soften the dried bread in a little cold water, then reduce it to coarse crumbs. Put the breadcrumbs, tomatoes, spring onions, yellow pepper, garlic, olives and basil leaves in a bowl and mix well. Add the olive oil and vinegar and season with salt and pepper. Mix very well to obtain a moist but not too wet mixture. Serve garnished with the anchovies and a sprig of basil.

stuffed baby artichokes
carciofini ripieni

The origin of this recipe must come from the Jewish ghetto in Rome where kosher food was the rule. These are popular with a lot of my Jewish friends. During cooking, the artichokes should be practically covered with olive oil but that is an expensive way of using the oil. Alternatively you can put 1 cm (½ in) in the bottom of the pan and then add sufficient water to push the level of the oil higher. This allows the temperature to be controlled more easily. Three per person is a wonderful starter and they are very good as part of an *antipasto*.

SERVES 4

12 BABY ARTICHOKES
JUICE 1 LEMON

FOR THE STUFFING
120 G (4½ OZ) STALE WHITE BREADCRUMBS
150 ML (5 FL OZ) MILK
1 TABLESPOON FINELY CHOPPED FRESH FLAT-LEAF PARSLEY
¼ GARLIC CLOVE, CRUSHED
1 TABLESPOON FRESHLY GRATED PARMESAN
½ TABLESPOON DRAINED CAPERS
LARGE PINCH SEA SALT AND FRESHLY GROUND BLACK PEPPER
EXTRA VIRGIN OLIVE OIL

METHOD

Trim the artichokes, cutting off the top third and trimming round the base to remove all the tough leaves. Cut out any choke, making a hollow in the centre which will hold the stuffing. Plunge into a bowl of water acidulated with lemon juice to prevent discoloration.

   Meanwhile, soak the breadcrumbs with the milk and squeeze out the moisture with your hands. Mix with the remaining stuffing ingredients. Fill the artichokes with the stuffing and pack side-by-side in a pan. The size of the pan is important as the artichokes must fit closely together. Drizzle the artichokes with a thin stream of olive oil and fill the base of the pan with 1 cm (½ in) depth. Add water to within 1 cm (½ in) of the top of the artichokes. Cover with a lid and simmer for about 20–30 minutes until tender. They are cooked when a knife pierces the artichokes easily. Cool a little and serve.

rolled sun-dried tomatoes
rotoli di pomodori secchi

Choose very large sun-dried tomatoes for this dish in order to roll them up with the filling. Sun-dried tomatoes can be used in various ways or enjoyed plain as a snack. However, they are quite salty so it is best to soak them before use in two parts vinegar to one part water for an hour or so, then drain and pat dry. They can then be flavoured with basil, oregano, garlic or chilli and covered with olive oil to be eaten later on. Alternatively, try this recipe.

MAKES 20

20 LARGE SUN-DRIED TOMATOES (LEAVE THE HALVES OF EACH
   TOMATO ATTACHED)

1 TEASPOON DRIED OREGANO

4 TABLESPOONS EXTRA VIRGIN OLIVE OIL

1 TABLESPOON SALTED CAPERS, SOAKED IN WATER FOR 10 MINUTES,
   THEN DRAINED

1 TABLESPOON MINT LEAVES

20 ANCHOVY FILLETS IN OIL

METHOD

Desalt and soften the sun-dried tomatoes as described above. Sprinkle them with the oregano and olive oil. Open out the tomato halves and place a few capers, mint leaves and an anchovy fillet in each tomato. Roll up to enclose the filling. Spear each roll with a cocktail stick to serve.

chicken liver crostini
crostini di fegatini

This recipe is so good that it is worth making double the quantity so that you have some in reserve – you can always use it for little snacks. *Crostini* are a favourite appetizer which originates in Tuscany, where they use not only chicken livers but also game birds and wild boar to produce an enviable array of pâtés. Imagine you are leaning back on a wooden chair under a pergola in a hilly part of Tuscany, where you have one of those views of typical Italian landscapes painted by an Italian old master. In your left hand you have a fresh *crostino* and in your right a nice glass of young Chianti. You have the right mix of ingredients to forget the cares of the world.

SERVES 4

2 TABLESPOONS EXTRA VIRGIN OLIVE OIL

1 MEDIUM ONION, FINELY CHOPPED

300 G (11 OZ) CHICKEN LIVERS

2 LARGE SPRIGS FRESH ROSEMARY

2 TABLESPOONS DRY WHITE WINE

2 LARGE ANCHOVY FILLETS

½ TABLESPOON CAPERS, DRAINED

4 TABLESPOONS CHICKEN STOCK

FRESHLY GROUND BLACK PEPPER

SEA SALT

100 G (4 OZ) UNSALTED BUTTER

12 THIN SLICES OF CRUSTY WHITE ITALIAN BREAD,
   10 CM (4 IN) IN DIAMETER

METHOD

First, wash and trim the chicken livers. Fry the onion gently in the olive oil for 5 minutes until soft but not coloured. Add the livers and one sprig of rosemary and cook gently, stirring from time to time, for approximately 8 minutes until the livers are cooked. Add the white wine, and allow the alcohol to evaporate for 2–3 minutes. Discard the sprig of rosemary and coarsely process in a food processor. Be careful, this will only take seconds!

Return the purée to the pan. Add the anchovy fillets, capers and chicken stock and cook gently for 2–3 minutes. Check the seasoning, adding lots of black pepper but probably only a little salt, if any, due to the saltiness of the anchovies and capers. Finally, stir in the butter. Keep the pâté warm while you toast the slices of bread. Spread them with pâté, arrange on a plate and garnish with the remaining sprig of rosemary.

raw beef alba-style
carne all'albese

There are various raw beef dishes, mostly called *carpaccio*. However, this recipe was created before that! Traditionally it is served with thinly sliced white Alba truffle which is available only between October and January. This is the summer version which uses asparagus though it is still called *Carne all'Albese*.

SERVES 4

400 G (14 OZ) MEDALLIONS OF VERY LEAN BEEF FILLET

8 TABLESPOONS EXTRA VIRGIN OLIVE OIL

4 TABLESPOONS LEMON JUICE

SALT AND PEPPER TO TASTE

THIN SLICES OF PARMESAN

ASPARAGUS TIPS, THINLY SLICED, OR THINLY SLICED WHITE TRUFFLE

METHOD

Place each medallion between sheets of clingfilm and beat with a mallet until thin. Layer the thin slices of beef to cover a plate. Top with the olive oil, lemon juice, salt and pepper and thin slices of Parmesan. Add the thin slices of asparagus or truffle.

courgette fritters
frittelle di zucchini

I made these once on the spur of the moment, when friends arrived unexpectedly and I didn't have anything to serve with drinks.

MAKES 24 FRITTERS

750 G (1¾ LB) COURGETTES, TOPPED, TAILED AND COARSELY GRATED

¼ LARGE GARLIC CLOVE, CRUSHED

3 EGGS, LIGHTLY BEATEN

2 TABLESPOONS FRESHLY GRATED PARMESAN

SEA SALT

FRESHLY GROUND BLACK PEPPER

PINCH FRESHLY GRATED NUTMEG

5 TABLESPOONS PLAIN FLOUR

2 TABLESPOONS FINELY CHOPPED FRESH MINT LEAVES

EXTRA VIRGIN OLIVE OIL FOR SHALLOW FRYING

METHOD

Mix all the ingredients together. Shallow-fry heaped tablespoons of the mixture in 1 cm (½ in) of hot oil until crisp and golden on both sides. Only turn over when a good crust has formed on the first side and work quickly because the salt added to the mixture will draw out the water from the courgettes. If you find that this happens, add a little more flour, but only as a last resort.

COURGETTE FRITTERS · SOUPS & STARTERS 17

stuffed peppers, aubergines and courgettes *peperoni, melanzane e zucchini ripieni*

This popular vegetable dish is served as a main course in Southern Italy, or as an *antipasto* or snack. Any vegetable that makes a suitable container can be stuffed with a variety of fillings. My mother always used to bake more stuffed vegetables than she needed and they made an excellent midnight feast when my brothers and I returned home and raided the fridge. This version is not for vegetarians, unless you omit the ham.

SERVES 4

1 YELLOW PEPPER

1 RED PEPPER

2 SMALL AUBERGINES

2 COURGETTES

200 G (7 OZ) STALE BREAD, CRUSTS REMOVED

1 EGG, BEATEN

3 TABLESPOONS FINELY CHOPPED FRESH PARSLEY

150 G (5 OZ) PARMA HAM, CUT INTO SMALL CUBES

1 GARLIC CLOVE, FINELY CHOPPED

150 G (5 OZ) CACIOCAVALLO CHEESE, CUT INTO SMALL CUBES

150 G (5 OZ) PECORINO CHEESE, CUT INTO SMALL CUBES

2 TABLESPOONS FRESHLY GRATED PARMESAN CHEESE

OLIVE OIL FOR DRIZZLING

SALT AND FRESHLY GROUND BLACK PEPPER

METHOD

Preheat the oven to 200°C/400°F/Gas Mark 6.

Cut the peppers in half down through the centre, including the stalk. Clean out the seeds and cut out the membranes with a sharp knife. Cut the aubergines and the courgettes in half lengthways and carefully scoop out the flesh (a melon baller is good for this), leaving a boat-shaped vegetable.

Soften the bread briefly in a little water and then squeeze it dry and make it into fine crumbs. Mix thoroughly with the egg, parsley, ham, garlic, cheeses and some salt and pepper. Fill the cavities of the vegetables with this mixture, packing it in loosely rather than pressing it down. Place the stuffed vegetables on an oiled baking tray, drizzle each one generously with olive oil and bake for 35 minutes, until the vegetables are tender and the filling is browned. Serve hot, warm or cold.

cardoon soup with chicken dumplings

zuppa di cardi e polpettine di pollo

Cardoon, a member of the thistle family, resembles a large head of celery and has long white fleshy ribs and silvery green leaves. It gives an extremely subtle taste to the broth. Like celery, the tender inner stalk is the best part of the vegetable, but you can also use the outer part with the stringy filaments removed. If you cannot find cardoons you can use celery instead.

SERVES 4

120 G (4½ OZ) SKINNED CHICKEN BREAST

5 TABLESPOONS FRESHLY GRATED PARMESAN

⅓ TEASPOON GARLIC OIL OR ½ GARLIC CLOVE VERY FINELY CHOPPED

PINCH FRESHLY GRATED NUTMEG

1 TABLESPOON FRESH WHITE BREADCRUMBS

1 EGG

1 TEASPOON CHOPPED FRESH FLAT-LEAF PARSLEY

SEA SALT

FRESHLY GROUND BLACK PEPPER

275 G (10 OZ) CARDOON OR CELERY STICKS

1.2 LITRES (2 PINTS) CHICKEN STOCK OR A BOUILLON CUBE

1 TEASPOON CHOPPED FRESH CHIVES

METHOD

Mince the chicken breast with 1 tablespoon of the Parmesan, the garlic, nutmeg, breadcrumbs, egg, parsley, salt and pepper in a food processor. Using 1 level dessertspoon of mixture for each dumpling, form into little balls with the palms of your hands, making 10 per person.

Strip the cardoon leaves from the stems, then peel the sticks to remove the outer strings and cut into 1 cm (½ in) pieces. Bring to the boil with the stock and simmer, adding the chicken dumplings after 10 minutes, until *al dente*. Add the chives, divide between the bowls and sprinkle with the remaining Parmesan.

braised lentils with borage
zuppa di lenticchie

The translation of *zuppa* as soup doesn't reflect the hearty nature of this lentil stew from Campania, which is one of several dishes from the area using the herb borage. Very simple, but very tasty indeed. Some people like to add a little chilli at the beginning but I prefer not to. Use Castelluccio lentils if you can get them, or Puy lentils.

SERVES 4

400 G (14 OZ) LENTILS

2 GARLIC CLOVES, PEELED BUT LEFT WHOLE

1.5 LITRES (2½ PINTS) CHICKEN OR VEGETABLE STOCK

200 G (7 OZ) CHERRY TOMATOES, HALVED

225 G (8 OZ) BORAGE LEAVES, ROUGHLY CHOPPED (SAVE THE BLUE
    FLOWERS FOR DECORATION)

120 ML (4 FL OZ) EXTRA VIRGIN OLIVE OIL

SALT AND FRESHLY GROUND BLACK PEPPER

METHOD

Put the lentils, garlic and stock in a pan, bring to the boil and simmer for 15 minutes. Add the tomatoes and borage leaves and continue to cook until the lentils are tender. Season with salt and pepper. Serve in soup bowls with the olive oil drizzled over and decorated with the borage flowers.

stuffed courgette flowers
fiori di zucchini ripieni

There are two types of courgette flowers. The one sold with the little courgette attached is the female. However, if you know a farmer or a keen gardener who grows courgettes, go and see him as he may give you male flowers, which are the ones attached to a stem without the courgette. I can still remember the face of Padre Emiliano, a very nice orthodox Catholic from Grotta Ferrata near Rome, when I invited him to come and eat some stuffed courgette flowers with me. I don't think he had ever eaten anything like them before. The expression on his face after tasting one or two was of complete beatitude. After courgette flowers, we went on to eat gnocchi with Gorgonzola cheese and my *tiramisù*, and later on, he had a huge steak as well! When I mentioned that he might perhaps have overdone it, he said with a smiling face that his work had been very hard that morning and that was his calorie reward!

SERVES 4

120 G (4½ OZ) SPINACH

135 G (4¾ OZ) FRESH RICOTTA CHEESE

4 TABLESPOONS CHOPPED FRESH BASIL

3 TABLESPOONS FRESHLY GRATED PARMESAN

2 EGGS

LARGE PINCH FRESHLY GRATED NUTMEG

SLICE OF 1 GARLIC CLOVE, CRUSHED

SEA SALT

FRESHLY GROUND BLACK PEPPER

8 COURGETTE FLOWERS

OIL FOR SHALLOW OR DEEP FRYING

METHOD

Wash the spinach well, cook, and allow to cool and squeeze to remove excess liquid. Mix the spinach, ricotta cheese, basil, Parmesan, 1 egg, nutmeg, garlic, salt and pepper together well. Using a piping bag, three-quarters fill each courgette flower. Beat the remaining egg and coat each flower with it. Shallow or deep fry the flowers until golden. Serve at once.

aunt dora's pasta and bean soup
pasta e fagiolo di zia dora

This soup is served all over Italy but it varies from region to region – almost from family to family. The main differences between the Northern and Southern versions are that in the South cannellini beans are used instead of borlotti and they are not crushed to thicken the soup. Also, Southern Italians make it with olive oil rather than other fats, which means the soup can be eaten cold, as is customary during summer. This recipe takes me back to wartime, when I used to spend my holidays with my favourite aunt, Dora, in the province of Avellino.

SERVES 4

300 G (11 OZ) FRESH CANNELLINI BEANS (OR 150 G/5 OZ DRIED BEANS,
  SOAKED IN WATER OVERNIGHT AND THEN DRAINED)
1.5 LITRES (2½ PINTS) STOCK (A CUBE WILL DO)
2 VERY RIPE SMALL TOMATOES, FINELY CHOPPED
4 TABLESPOONS VIRGIN OLIVE OIL
2 GARLIC CLOVES, ROUGHLY CHOPPED
4 BASIL LEAVES
300 G (11 OZ) TUBETTINI PASTA
SALT AND FRESHLY GROUND BLACK PEPPER
EXTRA VIRGIN OLIVE OIL FOR DRIZZLING

METHOD

Place the beans in a large pan with the stock and tomatoes and bring to the boil. Cover and simmer until the beans are tender (about 1½ –2 hours).

Heat the oil in a separate pan, add the garlic and fry until it is golden brown but not burnt. Stir this into the soup with the basil. Add the pasta and cook until the pasta is soft (not too *al dente* in this case). Serve with a drizzle of extra virgin olive oil, salt and plenty of black pepper.

If you use canned beans, start by frying the garlic in the oil, then add the tomatoes, stock and beans and bring to the boil. Add the pasta and basil and simmer until the pasta is cooked.

melon and parma ham soup
zuppa di melone e prosciutto

This is a wonderful way to enjoy Parma ham and melon and not only for toothless people! It adds another dimension to summer eating. The combination of a little orange and lemon juice gives it a special spiciness and, in summer, this is one of the bestsellers in my restaurant.

SERVES 4

1 VERY RIPE 1–1.5 KG (2¼–3 LB) CANTALOUPE OR CHARENTAIS
   MELON (ORANGE FLESH IS ESSENTIAL)

JUICE 1 ORANGE

JUICE ¼ LEMON

½ TEASPOON SEA SALT

½ TEASPOON COARSELY GROUND PINK PEPPERCORNS

SUGAR TO TASTE

4 LARGE SLICES PARMA HAM, CUT INTO THIN RIBBONS

METHOD

Peel and liquidize the melon to a coarse purée. Stir in the orange and lemon juices. Season with salt and pepper and add sugar to taste (this should not be necessary if the melon is ripe and flavourful). Mix in one quarter of the Parma ham and divide the soup between the four bowls. Sprinkle the remaining Parma ham onto the soup, with a final twist of the pepper grinder on top.

mussels taranto-style

cozze alla tarantina

High-quality mussels are cultivated in Taranto, the large Italian port in the Gulf of Taranto in Puglia. The flavour of these mussels is so good that you need add very few ingredients to make a great dish. Mussels are cooked in this way in other regions, too, where they are known as *Cozze Gratinate*. They can be eaten hot or cold and are delicious.

SERVES 4, OR MORE AS PART OF AN *ANTIPASTO*

1 KG (2¼ LB) MUSSELS

50 G (2 OZ) *AGLIO E MUDDICA* (SEE PAGE 27)

OLIVE OIL FOR DRIZZLING

4 TABLESPOONS TOMATO JUICE

4 TABLESPOONS DRY WHITE WINE

METHOD

Preheat the oven to 200°C/400°F/Gas Mark 6.

Scrub the mussels thoroughly under cold running water, pulling out the beards and discarding any open mussels that do not close when tapped on a work surface. Put the mussels in a large pan with 2 tablespoons of water. Cover and cook over a medium-high heat for 3–4 minutes, shaking the pan occasionally, until all the shells are open (discard any that remain closed).

Remove the top half of the shell from each mussel. Arrange the mussels in tightly packed rows on a baking tray and cover with the breadcrumb mixture (*Aglio e Muddica*). Drizzle with olive oil and bake for 8 minutes. Pour the tomato juice over the mussels and bake for a further 10 minutes. Pour over the white wine and bake for another 2 minutes.

aubergine rolls
involtini di melanzane

Aubergines are greatly enjoyed in Puglia, Calabria, Sicily and Basilicata, and naturally many recipes for them have developed. This is one of the simplest.

SERVES 4

12 LONG SLICES OF AUBERGINE, 5 MM (¼ IN) THICK

OLIVE OIL FOR FRYING

10 TABLESPOONS FRESH BREADCRUMBS, LIGHTLY TOASTED

12 OLIVES, PITTED AND COARSELY CHOPPED

6 TABLESPOONS COARSELY GRATED PECORINO CHEESE

1 TOMATO, VERY FINELY CHOPPED

12 BASIL LEAVES

SALT AND FRESHLY GROUND BLACK PEPPER

METHOD

Preheat the oven to 200°C/400°F/Gas Mark 6.

Cook the aubergine slices in boiling salted water for 2 minutes, then drain and pat dry. Heat some oil in a large frying pan and fry the aubergine slices until brown on both sides. Lay the slices out on a work surface.

Mix together the toasted breadcrumbs, olives, half the pecorino cheese and the tomato, then season to taste with salt and pepper. Spread the mixture over the aubergine slices, place a basil leaf on top of each one and roll up, securing the rolls with a wooden cocktail stick. Place the rolls on a baking tray, sprinkle the rest of the pecorino cheese over them and bake for 10 minutes. They can be eaten hot or cold.

poor man's parmesan
aglio e muddica

Like many peasant dishes, this owes its invention to poverty. It was devised as a cheap substitute for Parmesan cheese, which used to be a rather expensive commodity reserved for the rich. In fact it is known as Poor Man's Parmesan. Nowadays, though, *Aglio e Muddica* (garlic and breadcrumbs) offers a pleasant alternative to cheese and no longer deserves the name 'poor'. The crumbs are cunningly flavoured with a little olive oil, garlic and basil and are kept dry and crumbly like grated cheese. It is essential to use Southern-style rustic bread made with durum wheat flour. The mixture can be sprinkled on pasta dishes, vegetables, meat and anything else you think it may complement. Ideal for people with an allergy to dairy products.

MAKES 200 G (7 OZ)

200 G (7 OZ) FRESH BREADCRUMBS (BEST MADE FROM
  COUNTRY-STYLE BREAD THAT IS 1–2 DAYS OLD)
½ GARLIC CLOVE
1 TABLESPOON EXTRA VIRGIN OLIVE OIL
1 TABLESPOON VERY FINELY CHOPPED FRESH BASIL
SALT

METHOD

Rub the breadcrumbs through your fingers until they are the size of half a rice grain. Chop the garlic as finely as you can to obtain a paste, then mix it with the olive oil. Wet your fingers with a little of the oil and try to manipulate the breadcrumbs until all the oil has been incorporated and the crumbs become loose and not sticky. Add the basil and some salt and work with your fingers again to obtain a homogeneous mixture. Store in the fridge.

rice salad with three mushrooms
riso in insalata con tre funghi

Salad is something you usually associate with summer. For this dish, you have to choose a lovely late summer's day because you want to use wild mushrooms which are in the main available from the beginning of August to the end of October. I use the best risotto rice ever, carnaroli, not for the creaminess for which it is famous and which is normally the reason for choosing it, but for the big big grains which, being very absorbent, swell up and remain slightly *al dente*. For the mushrooms, you will need at least three different kinds, but you can use as many as you wish. At this time of year, you can find ceps, horn of plenty and oyster mushrooms but you should always check a reference book before picking them. If wild mushrooms are not available, the best replacements are the cultivated shiitake, oyster and button mushrooms, with the addition of some dried porcini for taste.

SERVES 4

10 G (¼ OZ) DRIED PORCINI

150 ML (5 FL OZ) TEPID WATER

200 G (7 OZ) RISOTTO RICE, CARNAROLI, VIALONE NANO OR ARBORIO

1 SMALL ONION, FINELY CHOPPED

2 TABLESPOONS EXTRA VIRGIN OLIVE OIL

250 G (9 OZ) MIXED MUSHROOMS, THINLY SLICED

1 TABLESPOON FINELY CHOPPED FRESH FLAT-LEAF PARSLEY

SEA SALT

FRESHLY GROUND BLACK PEPPER

FOR THE VINAIGRETTE

2 TABLESPOONS EXTRA VIRGIN OLIVE OIL

JUICE OF ½ LEMON

1 TABLESPOON FINELY CHOPPED FRESH FLAT-LEAF PARSLEY

2 TABLESPOONS CHOPPED FRESH CHIVES

SEA SALT

FRESHLY GROUND BLACK PEPPER

METHOD

Soak the dried porcini in the tepid water for 15 minutes, then squeeze dry, reserving the soaking liquor.

Simmer the rice in a large pan of boiling lightly salted water until *al dente*. Drain and, if the starch still remains, rinse with a kettle of boiling water. Meanwhile, fry the onion gently until soft without colouring. Add the fresh mushrooms, soaked porcini and parsley, together with a little salt to help extract the juices of the mushrooms. Mix the rice with the mushrooms, adding 2 tablespoons of the soaking liquor for moisture. Mix the vinaigrette ingredients together and stir into the rice. Adjust the seasoning and serve chilled.

2 pasta & rice

marille salad

marille in insalata

The Italian car styling genius, Giorgetto Giugiaro, was commissioned by an Italian pasta company to design an ergonomic, 'sauce-dynamic' pasta shape. According to him this was at a time when people were being encouraged to eat less pasta, so his aim was to design a shape that would hold a lot of sauce! He succeeded in creating on the drawing board a piece of edible sculpture which should certainly be included in the Agnesi pasta museum in Rome. This recipe produced by his personal chef, in salad, is excellent. Here, I prefer to use Taggiasca olives, which are very small and black.

SERVES 6

500 G (1 LB 2 OZ) MARILLE

6 TABLESPOONS OLIVE OIL

350 G (12 OZ) CHERRY TOMATOES

20 G (¾ OZ) FRESH BASIL

1 TABLESPOON SMALL CAPERS

50 G (2 OZ) BLACK OLIVES

2 TABLESPOONS COARSELY GRATED PARMESAN

METHOD

Bring a large saucepan of slightly salted water to the boil. Add the pasta and cook for about 10–12 minutes until *al dente*. Drain and put in a serving dish to cool and dress with 2 tablespoons of the olive oil.

Chop the tomatoes and basil. Add the capers, olives, the remaining olive oil and Parmesan and mix well with the pasta.

Keep chilled until ready to use, but not for more than one day.

spaghetti for pinuccia
spaghetti alla pinuccia

I created this recipe in honour of Pinuccia, the exceptional chef at the San Giovanni restaurant, in Casarza. I was incredibly impressed by her dedication in producing outstanding food with ingredients hunted personally on a daily basis. If you are in that area pay her a visit, it will be nicely rewarded. Use cooked king prawns if you can't get raw ones and reduce the cooking time slightly. Also, if you use tagliolini the pasta will take slightly less time to cook.

SERVES 4

400 G (14 OZ) UNCOOKED KING PRAWNS

6 TABLESPOONS OLIVE OIL

1 GARLIC CLOVE, CHOPPED

1 MEDIUM-SIZED RED CHILLI PEPPER, CHOPPED

1 TABLESPOON FRESH PARSLEY, CHOPPED

5 TABLESPOONS WHITE WINE

400 G (14 OZ) *POLPA DI POMODORO* (TOMATO PULP)

500 G (1 LB 2 OZ) SPAGHETTI OR FRESH EGG TAGLIOLINI

METHOD

Peel the central part of the prawns, leaving the head and tail shell intact. Heat the oil in a frying pan and add the garlic, chilli and parsley, taking care not to burn them. Then add the prawns and fry for a minute. Stir in the wine and the tomato pulp. Cook for a further 2–3 minutes.

Meanwhile, cook the pasta in slightly salted boiling water. If using fresh, cook for 2–3 minutes, if using the dried variety about 6–7 minutes.

Drain the pasta, add to the pan with the sauce, mix very well and serve immediately.

rice balls

arancini

One of the most popular rice specialities is the *Arancino di Riso*, which comes from Sicily and is now available everywhere. Sold as fast food in cafés and delicatessens, it is called *arancino* because it is the size and shape of an orange. There are two types, filled with either ragù or cheese. Ideally, they are best eaten fresh but, with the advent of microwaves in Italy, they are now usually served warmed up. Here is the cheese version.

MAKES 8

300 G (11 OZ) ARBORIO RICE
200 G (7 OZ) MIXTURE OF MOZZARELLA AND FRESH (*DOLCE*)
   PECORINO CHEESE, CUT INTO CUBES
50 G (2 OZ) PARMESAN CHEESE, FRESHLY GRATED
50 G (2 OZ) BUTTER, CUT INTO 8 CUBES
2 EGGS, BEATEN
DRIED BREADCRUMBS FOR COATING
PLENTY OF LARD OR OLIVE OIL FOR DEEP FRYING
SALT AND FRESHLY GROUND BLACK PEPPER

METHOD

Preheat the oven to 220°C/425°F/Gas Mark 7.

Cook the rice in boiling salted water for 12 minutes or until *al dente* and then drain. Mix the mozzarella and pecorino with the grated Parmesan and some black pepper.

Divide the rice into 8 equal parts. Wet your hands, then take a portion of the rice and line the palm of your hand with it, 2 cm (¾ in) thick, to make a mould that you can put the filling in. Place some of the cheese mixture and one cube of butter in the middle. Close your hand to make a ball, ensuring that the filling is completely enclosed by the rice. Press the rice together to shape the ball. Season the beaten eggs, then gently roll the rice balls in them. Next coat them completely in breadcrumbs and then deep fry in lard or olive oil over a medium heat until the *arancini* are golden. Place them in the oven for 8 minutes to brown them further and ensure the filling is melted, then serve immediately.

sardinian ravioli
culurzones

It is interesting that two regions as far apart as Sardinia and the Veneto have a very similar way of shaping their home-made ravioli. Although the fillings are different, they both taste wonderful. You need a little patience to make *culurzones* but the result is very rewarding. The great footballer Gianfranco Zola was delighted when I made this dish from his home town of Orlena in Sardinia as a surprise for him. Unfortunately, the setting was less traditional – the grounds of Chelsea Football Club.

SERVES 6-8

50 G (2 OZ) BUTTER

8 SAGE LEAVES

A PINCH OF SAFFRON, DISSOLVED IN A LITTLE HOT WATER

FRESHLY GRATED PECORINO OR PARMESAN CHEESE, TO SERVE

FOR THE FILLING

800 G (1¾ LB) POTATOES, BOILED AND MASHED

200 G (7 OZ) FRESH (*DOLCE*) PECORINO CHEESE, GRATED

50 G (2 OZ) AGED PECORINO CHEESE, GRATED

120 G (4½ OZ) PARMESAN CHEESE, FRESHLY GRATED

2½ TABLESPOONS EXTRA VIRGIN OLIVE OIL

2½ TABLESPOONS FINELY CHOPPED FRESH MINT

FOR THE DOUGH

300 G (11 OZ) *DOPPIO ZERO* (00) FLOUR

1 EGG YOLK

ABOUT 120 ML (4 FL OZ) WATER

METHOD

To make the filling, mix together the potatoes, three cheeses, oil and mint, then set to one side.

To make the dough, pile the flour up into a volcano shape on a work surface (marble is best) and make a large well in the centre. Put the egg yolk and water in the well, keeping back a little of the water in case you don't need it all. Lightly beat the egg yolk and water together with a fork and then gradually mix in the flour with your hands, adding a little more water if necessary, to make a soft dough. Knead the dough well with the palms of your hands for about 20 minutes, until smooth and elastic.

Roll out the pasta either by hand or with a pasta machine until it is very thin – about 2 mm ($\frac{1}{16}$ in). Cut out 10 cm (4 in) rounds. Knead the trimmings together, reroll and cut out more rounds.

To shape the *culurzones*, take a pasta round in one hand and place a teaspoonful of the filling mixture off-centre on it. Turn up the bottom of the dough over the filling, then pinch a fold of dough over from the right and then the left side to give a pleated effect. Pinch the top together to seal. You should end up with a money-bag shape. To prevent drying, it is important to work quickly and to keep the remaining pasta rounds covered.

Put the butter, sage leaves and saffron water in a large pan and heat gently until the butter has melted. Meanwhile, cook the *culurzones* in plenty of lightly salted boiling water until *al dente*. Drain and combine with the hot butter mixture, stirring to coat well. Serve either with more grated pecorino or with Parmesan, as you prefer.

open raviolo with mushrooms
raviolo aperto con funghi

Funghi – I always have to think of something special to say because I really like them: picking, eating and, naturally, preserving them. In this recipe, they look as though they are having a wonderful rest under a blanket, but only until you have dug in with the fork! Use porcini and chanterelles if they are in season, otherwise use mushrooms like the exotic shiitake, or button mushrooms combined with dried porcini. If using wild mushrooms, always consult a reference book first. Here I use ground almonds rather than cream to achieve a smooth creamy sauce.

SERVES 4

10 G (¼ OZ) DRIED PORCINI

FRESHLY MADE PASTA USING 100 G (4 OZ) STRONG WHITE PLAIN FLOUR
AND 1 EGG (SEE MASTER RECIPE PAGE 52)

65 G (2½ OZ) BUTTER

1 SMALL ONION, FINELY CHOPPED

300 G (11 OZ) MIXED FRESH WILD MUSHROOMS, CLEANED AND THINLY SLICED

1 TABLESPOON FINELY CHOPPED FRESH FLAT-LEAF PARSLEY

25 G (1 OZ) GROUND ALMONDS

6 TABLESPOONS MILK

SEA SALT

FRESHLY GROUND BLACK PEPPER

METHOD

Soak the dried porcini in 150 ml (¼ pint) water for 15 minutes, then squeeze dry, reserving the soaking liquor.

Either roll by hand, or use a pasta machine, to obtain 8 flat sheets of pasta measuring 15 x 15 cm (6 x 6 in). Cover with a clean tea towel. Meanwhile, in a large pan boil plenty of salted water.

In another pan, melt the butter and fry the onion gently until soft without colouring. Add the fresh mushrooms and soaked porcini to the pan, stirring, and fry for 2 minutes. Stir in the soaking liquor, parsley, ground almonds, milk, salt and pepper.

Simmer the pasta in the salted water until *al dente*. Drain and pat dry with kitchen paper. Place individual sheets on 4 warmed plates, spoon the mushrooms and their sauce on top (reserving a little for the final garnish) and cover with the remaining pasta sheets, folding the corner back, as if to prepare the bed for the night, exposing the filling. Add a little of the sauce and serve.

tagliolini with red mullet
tagliolini con triglie

Pinuccia, who cooks in the San Giovanni restaurant in Casarza, was a fishmonger before becoming a fantastic cook and perfectionist, and she knows all the tricks of the trade, and above all she never compromises about the freshness of fish. How wonderful to know that you are in the hands of a real professional. The *triglie di scoglio* which were used for the dish I ate there were caught that same morning.

SERVES 4

675 G (1½ LB) RED MULLET

3 TABLESPOONS OLIVE OIL

1 GARLIC CLOVE, CHOPPED

1 TABLESPOON PARSLEY, CHOPPED

5 TABLESPOONS WHITE WINE

SALT

250 G (9 OZ) *POLPA DI POMODORO* (TOMATO PULP)

500 G (1 LB 2 OZ) FRESH OR DRIED TAGLIOLINI

METHOD

Scale, gut and fillet the fish and cut into 5 cm (2 in) strips. Heat the oil in a frying pan. Fry the garlic, half the parsley and all the fish. Add the wine, stir well and cook for a couple of minutes. Season with salt and add the tomato pulp. Sprinkle with the remaining parsley and cook for a further 2–3 minutes.

Bring a large pan of slightly salted water to the boil. Add the tagliolini. If you are using fresh pasta, cook for about 2–3 minutes. If you are using the dried variety, cook for 6–8 minutes.

When cooked, drain the pasta and add to the sauce. Sauté for a short time on the heat to coat well. Serve immediately.

strangozzi norcia-style
strangozzi alla norcina

Norcia is more or less the capital of the black truffle and when you say a dish is 'alla Norcina', you will probably find truffles in it. Strangozzi are a typical Umbrian pasta made from durum wheat flour and water. The ribbons offer a certain consistency even after cooking because of their thickness and their shape, which is more square than flat. Combined with something as delicate and noble as the truffle, the result is outstanding. You can use tagliatelle instead if strangozzi are unavailable.

SERVES 4

1 GARLIC CLOVE

75 G (3 OZ) BUTTER

50 G (2 OZ) WHITE TRUFFLE

400 G (14 OZ) STRANGOZZI, FRESH OR DRIED

50 G (2 OZ) PARMESAN

FRESHLY GROUND BLACK PEPPER TO TASTE

METHOD

Rub a frying pan with the clove of garlic cut in half to allow the juices to flavour it and then discard. Heat the butter and pepper gently. Thinly shave three quarters of the truffle into the butter and keep warm without frying.

Meanwhile cook the pasta in plenty of water for 10–12 minutes (or less if the pasta is freshly made). Drain the pasta, toss in the pan with the sauce, add the Parmesan and serve with a few shavings of the remaining quarter of truffle.

spaghetti carbonara
spaghetti alla carbonara

I include a recipe for this well-known dish because most people I know get it completely wrong, either adding milk or cream or letting the eggs become scrambled. This recipe is the real thing. It was brought to Lazio from Umbria by coal men (*carbonari*), who came to sell charcoal to the Romans. Since then it has been adopted by the Romans and is famous worldwide.

SERVES 6

500 G (1 LB 2 OZ) SPAGHETTI OR SPAGHETTONI (THE LARGEST SPAGHETTI)

25 G (1 OZ) LARD

25 G (1 OZ) BUTTER

2 TABLESPOONS OLIVE OIL

1 GARLIC CLOVE, SLIGHTLY SQUASHED

100 G (4 OZ) PANCETTA OR *GUANCIALE* (SEE PAGE 7), CUT INTO SMALL CHUNKS

5 TABLESPOONS DRY WHITE WINE

5 EGGS

100 G (4 OZ) PARMESAN CHEESE (OR PECORINO FOR THE PURISTS), FRESHLY GRATED

3 TABLESPOONS FINELY CHOPPED FRESH PARSLEY

SALT AND FRESHLY GROUND BLACK PEPPER

METHOD

Cook the pasta in a large pan of boiling salted water until *al dente*. Meanwhile, heat the lard, butter and oil in a pan and fry the garlic and pancetta or *guanciale* until crisp. Discard the garlic and add the white wine to the pan. Boil to evaporate it a little.

Lightly beat the eggs in a large bowl with the grated cheese, parsley and some salt and pepper. When the pasta is ready, drain and add to the pancetta or *guanciale* in the pan. Stir a couple of times and add the egg mixture. Stir off the heat just to coat the pasta and serve.

bolognese sauce
ragù bolognese

One of the best known Italian recipes abroad, *Spaghetti Bolognese* does not exist in Italy. You will find it in restaurants run by non-Italians or by Italians not in touch with genuine Italian food. The real thing is called *Tagliatelle al Ragù* and comes from Bologna in Emilia Romagna. Genuine *Ragù Bolognese* is a mixture of at least two types of meat, like lean minced beef and pork, plus oil and butter, a little wine, an onion, plump ripe tomatoes and tomato paste. The sprinkling of freshly grated Parmesan perfectly crowns this very Emilian dish.

SERVES 4

25 G (1 OZ) BUTTER

2 TABLESPOONS OLIVE OIL

1 MEDIUM-SIZED ONION, CHOPPED

250 G (9 OZ) MINCED BEEF

250 G (9 OZ) MINCED PORK

6 TABLESPOONS WHITE WINE

1 KG (2 LB) *POLPA DI POMODORO* (TOMATO PULP)

1 TEASPOON CONCENTRATED TOMATO PURÉE

SALT AND FRESHLY GROUND BLACK PEPPER

METHOD

Heat the oil and butter in a pan and fry the chopped onion. Then add the meat and fry until golden brown. Stir in the wine, tomato pulp and tomato purée. Season with salt and pepper to taste. Cover with a lid and leave to simmer for about 2 hours, stirring from time to time.

Serve with freshly cooked tagliatelle and sprinkle with freshly grated Parmesan, if desired, but purists like this dish without.

trofie with pesto
trofie al pesto

Trofie is a particular pasta shape from Liguria. It is usually home-made but you can find it in good Italian shops. Alternatively use strozzapreti or fusilli instead.

SERVES 4

4 GARLIC CLOVES

40-50 FRESH BASIL LEAVES

10 G (¼ OZ) COARSE SEA SALT

50 G (2 OZ) PINE KERNELS

EXTRA VIRGIN OLIVE OIL, AS REQUIRED

50 G (2 OZ) FRESHLY GRATED PARMESAN

500 G (1 LB 2 OZ) DRIED TROFIE OR STROZZAPRETI OR FUSILLI

BASIL LEAVES, TO GARNISH

METHOD

Put the garlic and basil leaves in a mortar and add the salt, which under the pestle and the power of your elbow will function as a grinder. Also add the pine kernels and reduce to a paste, slowly drizzling in some olive oil. Incorporate the Parmesan and continue to grind with the pestle adding enough oil to achieve a very smooth and homogenous sauce of a brilliant green colour.

Boil the pasta in slightly salted water according to the instructions on the packet. Drain, transfer to a pre-warmed china bowl and mix thoroughly with the pesto. Decorate with some basil leaves and serve immediately. The sauce should cover each piece of pasta and there should be none left on the plate!

risotto with lentils and sausages
risotto con lenticchie e salamini

This dish is produced in various ways and is typical of the Vercelli area and Novara, the main commercial centre of Italian rice cultivation. Traditionally you would use rice from the last harvest and the first sausage made with a newly killed pig. They also make a very delicious version there with frogs, but I discovered they were very difficult to catch so here I have used little salamini instead. This is a one-course meal, the quantity is abundant and it is a dish to enjoy on a day when you are really hungry. If you do not have lentils, you can use beans or chickpeas.

SERVES 4

200 G (7 OZ) GREEN LENTILS

400 G (14 OZ) SALAMINI (LUGANIGA TYPE)

1 BAY LEAF

2.25 LITRES (4 PINTS) CHICKEN STOCK OR A BOUILLON CUBE

1 SMALL ONION, FINELY CHOPPED

5 TABLESPOONS EXTRA VIRGIN OLIVE OIL

200 G (7 OZ) POTATOES, PEELED AND CUT INTO 5 MM (¼ IN) DICE

2 STICKS CELERY, WASHED AND CUT INTO 5 MM (¼ IN) DICE

2 CARROTS, PEELED AND CUT INTO 5 MM (¼ IN) DICE

2 RIPE TOMATOES, CHOPPED, OR 2 TABLESPOONS *POLPA DI POMODORO*
   (TOMATO PULP)

320 G (11½ OZ) RISOTTO RICE (CARNAROLI, VIALONE NANO OR ARBORIO)

SEA SALT

FRESHLY GROUND BLACK PEPPER

METHOD

In a saucepan, simmer the lentils, salamini and bay leaf in the chicken stock for 15 minutes, covered.

In the meantime, fry the onion gently in the oil until soft but without colouring. Add the potatoes, celery, carrots and tomatoes and fry gently for 2 minutes. Add the risotto rice and stir to coat each grain. Stir in 1 ladleful of broth, lentils and sausages to the rice at a time, and continue to stir, allowing each ladleful to be absorbed into the rice grains before more is added. Continue until all is incorporated, when the rice should be creamy but still retain some bite. Check the seasoning and serve.

sardinian risotto

risotto sardo

This risotto does not differ much in principle from the Spanish *paella*. Considering that Sardinia and Catalonia have many things in common, including some dialect, this is not so surprising. It is, however, very different from the Northern Italian risotto.

SERVES 6

6 TABLESPOONS OLIVE OIL

600 G (1 LB 5 OZ) RISOTTO RICE

75 G (3 OZ) AGED PECORINO CHEESE, GRATED

40 G (1½ OZ) BUTTER

FRESHLY GROUND BLACK PEPPER

FOR THE RAGÙ

4 TABLESPOONS OLIVE OIL

1 SMALL ONION, FINELY CHOPPED

250 G (9 OZ) MINCED LEAN PORK OR VEAL

1 SMALL GLASS OF RED WINE (PREFERABLY SARDINIAN CANNONAU)

200 ML (7 FL OZ) CHICKEN STOCK

200 G (7 OZ) *POLPA DI POMODORO* (TOMATO PULP)

¼ TEASPOON GOOD SAFFRON POWDER

SALT

METHOD

First make the ragù. Heat the oil in a pan, add the onion and fry gently until softened. Then add the minced meat and fry until brown. Stir in the wine, stock, tomato pulp, saffron and some salt and simmer for 20–25 minutes. Remove from the heat and set the ragù aside.

For the risotto, heat the oil in a pan, add the rice and stir for about 5 minutes over a gentle heat to coat each grain with oil. Gradually add half the ragù and stir for 5 minutes. Keep an eye on the moisture level and add some hot water if necessary; the rice will absorb a lot of liquid. Add the rest of the ragù and stir for 10 minutes or until the rice is cooked. The consistency should be quite loose. Stir in the grated cheese, butter and some pepper. Leave to rest for a few minutes and then serve.

pumpkin risotto

risotto di zucca

This recipe comes from the Hotel Cipriani in Venice, a very welcoming place though rather pricey! Its food, unlike that at many other 'international' hotels, reflects local eating habits, something I very much approve of. The pumpkin is undergoing quite a revival at the moment and Renato Piccolotto, the hotel's chef, cooks this wonderful risotto, which is as appealing to the eye as it is to the palate. It is very simple to make but, like all simple and delicate things, requires a little attention. Pumpkins are now widely available and can even be bought in chunks.

SERVES 4

2 TABLESPOONS OLIVE OIL

90 G (3½ OZ) BUTTER

4 SPRIGS ROSEMARY, 2 FINELY CHOPPED AND 2 WHOLE

1 GARLIC CLOVE, WHOLE

600 G (1 LB 6 OZ) PUMPKIN FLESH, CHOPPED INTO VERY SMALL CHUNKS

1 SMALL ONION, FINELY CHOPPED

300 G (11 OZ) CARNAROLI RICE

1 LITRE (1¾ PINTS) CHICKEN STOCK

50 G (2 OZ) PARMESAN

SALT AND FRESHLY GROUND BLACK PEPPER

METHOD

In a pan, heat the oil and a third of the butter, add the sprigs of rosemary, garlic and the pumpkin. The pumpkin will automatically exude some liquid and so no water needs to be added. Cook for about 20 minutes or until the pumpkin softens and dissolves. Remove the rosemary sprigs and garlic clove.

In another large pan, heat half the remaining butter and fry the onion gently until soft, add the rice and stir-fry for a few minutes. Add a little of the chicken stock and then the pumpkin mixture. Add more stock until it is all used and absorbed by the rice, stirring from time to time to avoid sticking to the pan.

Take off the heat and beat in the remaining butter and the Parmesan and sprinkle with the chopped rosemary. If you have a spare pumpkin, deseed, warm inside with hot water, drain, fill with the risotto and serve.

risotto with two artichokes
risotto con due carciofi

The combination of the two artichokes gives this risotto an extremely delicate flavour. It is suitable for anything from a *piatto unico* (one-course meal) to one of the courses of an extremely elegant dinner party.

SERVES 4

4 x 50 G (2 OZ) SMALL GLOBE ARTICHOKES (TRIMMED WEIGHT) OR
 HEARTS FROM 4 LARGE FRESH GLOBE ARTICHOKES
600 ML (1 PINT) CHICKEN OR VEGETABLE STOCK OR A BOUILLON CUBE
1 SMALL ONION, FINELY CHOPPED
4 TABLESPOONS EXTRA VIRGIN OLIVE OIL
100 G (4 OZ) UNSALTED BUTTER
320 G (11½ OZ) JERUSALEM ARTICHOKES, PEELED, THINLY SLICED
350 G (12 OZ) RISOTTO RICE (CARNAROLI, VIALONE NANO OR ARBORIO)
50 G (2 OZ) FRESHLY GRATED PARMESAN
2 TEASPOONS FINELY CHOPPED FRESH FLAT-LEAF PARSLEY
SEA SALT
FRESHLY GROUND BLACK PEPPER

METHOD

Cut each small globe artichoke, or the artichoke hearts, in half and slice thinly. Bring the stock to the boil. Meanwhile, in a separate pan, fry the onion gently in the oil and 65 g (2½ oz) of the butter until soft without colouring. Add the globe and Jerusalem artichokes and lightly brown over a moderate heat. Add a little stock and braise for 2 minutes. Add the risotto rice and stir until each grain is coated. Gradually add the stock until it is absorbed and the grains are soft but still have a bite to them. Off the heat, stir in the Parmesan, the remaining butter and the parsley. Check the seasoning and serve.

cart drivers' spaghetti
spaghetti alla carrettiera

Together with pizza, spaghetti is the symbol of Naples. To celebrate artisan spaghetti, here is a curious recipe that not only the Neapolitans but also the Sicilians and Romans claim as their own. The Neapolitan version is very simple and is named in honour of the cart drivers who used to deliver food and wine to big cities. I find the combination of porcini and tuna quite intriguing.

SERVES 4

25 G (1 OZ) DRIED PORCINI MUSHROOMS

4 TABLESPOONS OLIVE OIL

1 GARLIC CLOVE, CRUSHED

50 G (2 OZ) PANCETTA, FINELY CHOPPED

200 G (7 OZ) CAN OF TUNA IN OIL, DRAINED

600 G (1 LB 5 OZ) *POMODORINI* (VERY SWEET CHERRY TOMATOES), CHOPPED, OR 500 G (1 LB 2 OZ) *POLPA DI POMODORO*

400 G (14 OZ) NEAPOLITAN SPAGHETTI

SALT

FRESHLY GROUND BLACK PEPPER (OPTIONAL)

FRESHLY GRATED PARMESAN CHEESE, TO SERVE (OPTIONAL)

METHOD

Soak the porcini in warm water for 30 minutes, then drain and chop, reserving the soaking liquid.

Heat the olive oil in a frying pan, add the garlic and fry gently until softened. Add the pancetta and allow to brown a little. Stir in the porcini and tuna and fry for a few minutes, then add the tomatoes and some salt and simmer for 20 minutes. Stir in a few spoonfuls of the mushroom soaking liquid just to flavour the sauce and cook for about 5 minutes longer.

Meanwhile, cook the spaghetti in a large pan of boiling salted water until *al dente*, then drain and mix with the sauce. Season with black pepper and sprinkle with Parmesan cheese.

pasta with mussels

cavatelli con le cozze

A speciality of Puglia and particularly of Bari, where cavatelli are still hand-made for special occasions from hard durum wheat semolina flour and water. You can buy high-quality commercially manufactured cavatelli in any good delicatessen. As it is quite soupy, this pasta dish may be eaten with a spoon.

SERVES 4

1 KG (2¼ LB) MUSSELS

6 TABLESPOONS EXTRA VIRGIN OLIVE OIL, PLUS EXTRA TO SERVE

1 GARLIC CLOVE, FINELY CHOPPED

1 SMALL CHILLI, FINELY DICED

300 G (11 OZ) CHERRY TOMATOES

1 SMALL BUNCH OF FLAT-LEAF PARSLEY, FINELY CHOPPED

400 G (14 OZ) CAVATELLI PASTA

SALT AND FRESHLY GROUND BLACK PEPPER

METHOD

Scrub the mussels thoroughly under cold running water, pulling out the beards and discarding any open mussels that do not close when tapped on a work surface. Put the mussels in a large pan with 2 tablespoons of water, cover and cook over a medium-high heat for 3–4 minutes, shaking the pan occasionally, until all the shells are open (discard any that remain closed). Remove the shells from half the mussels. Strain the cooking juices through a very fine sieve and set to one side.

Heat the oil in a frying pan, add the garlic and chilli and fry gently until the garlic is softened but not browned. Cut some of the cherry tomatoes in half. Add the halved and the whole tomatoes to the pan and fry until softened. Add the mussels, their cooking juices and the parsley and heat through gently. Season with salt and pepper to taste.

Meanwhile, cook the pasta in a large pan of lightly salted boiling water until *al dente*. Drain and stir into the mussel sauce. I like to pour a stream of extra virgin olive oil on to each portion for extra flavour.

fresh pasta
pasta all'uovo

This recipe is the basis for all types of home-made pasta. The best flour to use is '00' made from very finely milled tender wheat. When eggs are added, it gives the cooked pasta the 'crunchiness' much desired by Italians. You may also need to add a little durum wheat semolina if you want to make special shapes like trofie. Standard tagliatelle are made with about 6 whole eggs per kilo of flour, plus a little water if required. Sometimes, for example if you are making ravioli, pansotti or other filled pasta, you will want a softer more workable pasta dough and this can be achieved by using about 3 eggs and the necessary water to a kilo of flour.

The important thing to remember when making pasta is to work the dough well with a lot of elbow grease and then to rest it for an hour before using it. Then, once you have rolled and cut the dough to the required shape, leave it to dry for half an hour or so on a clean cloth. Homemade pasta cannot be kept for long because of its egg content. You should not refrigerate it – the best thing is to freeze it, though this will of course have an adverse effect on the quality of the finished dish. Bought dried pasta is dried industrially for 12 hours in special machines. Never add oil to the water when cooking pasta except for large squares of pasta like open ravioli. Never rinse pasta in cold water – if you want to cool it down and interrupt the cooking process, add a couple of glasses of cold water to the pot when you take it off the stove. In the restaurant of the Slow Food Society, I had some quite sensational pasta made with 40 – yes, 40! – egg yolks per kilo of flour.

MAKES ABOUT 450 G (1 LB) PASTA

300 G (11 OZ) DURUM WHEAT FLOUR OR PLAIN FLOUR, OR A MIXTURE OF BOTH
3 EGGS, SIZE 3 OR 4
PINCH OF SALT

METHOD

Sift the flour on to a clean work surface (marble is ideal), forming it into a volcano-shaped mound with a well in the centre. Break the eggs into the well and add the salt. Incorporate the eggs into the flour with your hands, gradually drawing the flour into the egg mixture until it forms a coarse paste. Add a little more flour if the mixture is too soft or sticky and, with a spatula, scrape up any pieces of dough. Before kneading the dough, clean your hands and the work surface. Lightly flour the work surface, and start to knead with the heel of one hand. Work the dough for 10–15 minutes until the consistency is smooth and elastic. Wrap the dough in clingfilm or foil and allow it to rest for half an hour.

Again, lightly flour your work surface, and a rolling pin. Gently roll the dough out, rotating it in quarter turns. Roll out the dough to a sheet 3 mm (⅛ in) in thickness. If you are making filled pasta, go straight ahead and incorporate the filling as in the recipes. If you are making flat pasta or shapes, leave the pasta on a clean tea towel to dry for about half an hour.

baked pasta
pasta al forno

This is a dish for grand occasions, such as weddings or Christmas. The pasta itself is only a vehicle for all sorts of goodies, resulting in a rich timbale. The curious thing is that at festive events it is customary to enjoy richer food than usual anyway, and so only a small wedge of this dish is eaten. The rest makes a welcome leftover the following evening. Some gourmet Neapolitans add fresh truffles but I think that is going a little too far...

SERVES 8

800 G (1¾ LB) PASTA, SUCH AS MACCHERONI, ZITI OR PENNE

450 G (1 LB) MOZZARELLA CHEESE, CUT INTO SMALL CUBES

200 G (7 OZ) PARMESAN CHEESE, FRESHLY GRATED

FOR THE SAUCE

100 ML (3½ FL OZ) OLIVE OIL

1 ONION, FINELY CHOPPED

1 GARLIC CLOVE, FINELY CHOPPED

500 G (1 LB 2 OZ) CHICKEN LIVERS AND HEARTS

400 G (14 OZ) FRESH PORCINI, CHOPPED, OR 400 G (14 OZ) OF
   CULTIVATED MUSHROOMS PLUS 25 G (1 OZ) DRIED PORCINI,
   SOAKED IN WARM WATER FOR 30 MINUTES, THEN DRAINED

1 SMALL GLASS OF WHITE WINE

1 KG (2¼ LB) RIPE TOMATOES, DESEEDED AND CHOPPED,
   OR 800 G (1¾ LB) *POLPA DI POMODORO*

2 TABLESPOONS CHOPPED FRESH BASIL

SALT AND FRESHLY GROUND BLACK PEPPER

METHOD

To make the sauce, heat the oil in a large pan and fry the onion and garlic until softened. Add the chicken livers and hearts and cook over a medium heat for 15 minutes, stirring all the time. Add the mushrooms and cook for a few minutes. Pour in the wine and boil to evaporate a little. Add the tomatoes and basil and cook gently for 40 minutes. Season to taste.

Preheat the oven to 200°C/400°F/Gas Mark 6.

Cook the pasta in a large pan of boiling salted water for half its normal cooking time, then drain and mix with a little of the sauce. Take a round or square 25–30 cm (10–12 in) baking tin or ovenproof dish about 7.5 cm (3 in) deep and, commencing with pasta, build layers of pasta and sauce, scattering mozzarella cubes and grated Parmesan in between. Finish with sauce and Parmesan cheese. Bake for 25 minutes and then serve.

orecchiette with broccoli and ham
orecchiette con broccoli e prosciutto

The purists of Puglian cuisine will be horrified at my audacity in adding ham to the classic dish *Orecchiette con Cime di Rape* and substituting broccoli for turnip tops. However, I find that this makes an extremely good combination and is still in keeping with the cuisine of the region.

SERVES 4

6 TABLESPOONS OLIVE OIL

50 G (2 OZ) PROSCIUTTO, CUT INTO SMALL CUBES

1 GARLIC CLOVE, FINELY CHOPPED

½ CHILLI, FINELY CHOPPED

6 SMALL CHERRY TOMATOES, QUARTERED

200 G (7 OZ) BROCCOLI FLORETS

2 TABLESPOONS FINELY CHOPPED FRESH PARSLEY

400 G (14 OZ) ORECCHIETTE

40 G (1½ OZ) PECORINO CHEESE, GRATED (OPTIONAL)

SALT AND FRESHLY GROUND BLACK PEPPER

METHOD

Heat the oil in a pan, add the prosciutto and fry for a few minutes. Add the garlic, chilli and tomatoes and fry briefly, then stir in the broccoli florets and a little water. Cover the pan and cook gently until the broccoli is tender, then stir in the parsley.

Meanwhile, cook the pasta in a large pan of lightly salted boiling water for 12–15 minutes, until *al dente*. Drain and add to the sauce. Mix well and season with salt and pepper. Serve with the pecorino cheese, if desired.

baked chickpea gnocchi

panelle al forno

Although this is similar in principle to *Gnocchi alla Romana*, I find that chickpea flour makes much tastier gnocchi than semolina. In Palermo, where *panelle* are fried and eaten sandwiched in bread, they would undoubtedly approve.

SERVES 4

1.5 LITRES (2½ PINTS) WATER

15 G (½ OZ) SALT

2 TABLESPOONS COARSELY CHOPPED FRESH PARSLEY

250 G (9 OZ) CHICKPEA FLOUR

50 G (2 OZ) BUTTER

1 TEASPOON FRESHLY GRATED NUTMEG

40 G (1½ OZ) PARMESAN CHEESE, FRESHLY GRATED

FRESHLY GROUND BLACK PEPPER

METHOD

Put the water in a pan with the salt and parsley and bring to the boil. Gradually pour in the chickpea flour, beating vigorously with a wire whisk to prevent lumps forming. Cook for 5 minutes, stirring, then pour the mixture on to an oiled surface and spread out in a layer 1 cm (½ in) thick. Leave to cool and set.

Preheat the oven to 200°C/400°F/Gas Mark 6.

Cut the chickpea mixture into circles 4 cm (1½ in) in diameter and arrange them on an oiled baking tray, overlapping them slightly. Dot with the butter and sprinkle the nutmeg, Parmesan cheese and black pepper over the surface. Bake for 10 minutes, then place under a hot grill to brown the top.

I use up the bits of dough left after cutting out the circles by baking them with a fresh tomato and basil sauce. I hate throwing food away!

3 meat & poultry

pork escalope with red wine braciolette di maiale al vino rosso ■ **roast pork with potatoes and garlic** arrosto di maiale con patate all'aglio ■ **lamb nuggets on a skewer** spiedino di nocciole d'agnello ■ **lamb with fennel and marsala** agnello con finocchio al marsala ■ **lamb cutlets with artichokes** braciole d'abbacchio con carciofi ■ **stuffed lamb cutlets** costoline di agnello ripiene ■ **veal escalopes with marsala** scaloppine al marsala secco ■ **braised beef in nebbiolo wine** brasato al nebbiolo ■ **luganiga sausage in red wine** luganiga al vino rosso ■ **medallions of beef with mushrooms** medaglioni di manzo con funghi ■ **calf's liver with marsala** fegato al marsala ■ **graziella's chicken** pollo di graziella ■ **chicken scaloppine with herbs** scaloppine di pollo con erbe ■ **jewish chicken rissoles** ngozzamoddi or azmot ■ **roast goose** oca arrosto ■ **duck verdi-style** anitra alla verdi ■ **sardinian-style partridge** pernice alla sarda

pork escalope with red wine
braciolette di maiale al vino rosso

In Italy, *braciola* is an ambiguous word. In the South, it means a piece of meat on the bone while in other parts of Italy it is boned, rolled meat. To do this, you take a thinly cut piece of either pork escalope or fillet, beat it thin and then cut it to the right size so you can roll it up. If you do not have a wonderful *batticarne* (beater) then ask your butcher to do this for you.

SERVES 4

1.5 KG (3 LB) PORK FILLET, CUT INTO 12 x 5 MM (¼ IN) SLICES

SEA SALT

FRESHLY GROUND BLACK PEPPER

20 G (¾ OZ) FRESHLY GRATED PARMESAN

2 TABLESPOONS FINELY CHOPPED FRESH FLAT-LEAF PARSLEY

1 TABLESPOON CHOPPED FRESH ROSEMARY

12 FRESH SAGE LEAVES

75 G (3 OZ) BUTTER

120 G (4½ OZ) *MORTADELLA* SAUSAGE, CUT INTO 1 x 7.5 CM (½ x 3 IN) STICKS

6 BABY GHERKINS (PICKLED IN DILL), CUT IN HALF

1 TABLESPOON EXTRA VIRGIN OLIVE OIL

1 RED PEPPER, SEEDED

200 ML (7 FL OZ) DRY RED WINE

1 SPRIG FRESH ROSEMARY

25 G (1 OZ) PLAIN FLOUR

METHOD

Place each slice of pork fillet between 2 sheets of clingfilm and beat with a mallet until thin. Season with salt and pepper, sprinkle with Parmesan, parsley, rosemary and sage. Dot with 25 g (1 oz) of butter and place a stick of *mortadella* and half a gherkin on each. Roll up each escalope and secure with a cocktail stick.

Heat 25 g (1 oz) of the butter and the oil and brown the pork evenly and quickly over a moderate heat. Add half the pepper which you have finely diced and fry for 2 minutes. Stir in the wine and cook for 2 minutes to evaporate the alcohol. Reduce the heat and add the sprig of rosemary. Combine the remaining 25 g (1 oz) butter and flour in a small bowl and whisk into the sauce. Adjust the seasoning and transfer the *braciolette* to plates, removing the cocktail sticks and spooning over the sauce.

Garnish with slices of the remaining half red pepper.

roast pork with potatoes and garlic

arrosto di maiale con patate all'aglio

Roast pork always makes a welcome meal for any lover of good food. The taste is distinctive and, when it is accompanied by complementary flavours such as garlic and rosemary, you can't go wrong. My favourite cut is the loin, which has enough skin to make plenty of delicious crackling.

SERVES 8

3 KG (7 LB) LOIN OF PORK

150 ML (5 FL OZ) OLIVE OIL

1.5 KG (3¼ LB) SMALL NEW POTATOES

10 GARLIC CLOVES, UNPEELED

4 SPRIGS OF ROSEMARY

SALT AND FRESHLY GROUND BLACK PEPPER

METHOD

Preheat the oven to 200°C/400°F/Gas Mark 6.

Score the pork skin with a small, sharp knife in order to make crackling. Rub the whole joint with some of the olive oil and with salt and pepper. Place in a large roasting tin, cover with aluminium foil and roast for 30 minutes. Add the potatoes, garlic and rosemary sprigs to the tin. Drizzle with the remaining olive oil, season with salt and pepper and bake without the foil for another 1½ hours, basting occasionally. Test the meat by piercing with a skewer; if the juices run clear it is done. Leave to rest for 15 minutes and then serve.

lamb nuggets on a skewer
spiedino di nocciole d'agnello

This dish always reminds me romantically of the natural, wild, gypsy life and brings back memories of cooking outside on hot summer days. A good roasted pepper salad with *crostini* is the ideal accompaniment.

SERVES 4

250 G (9 OZ) JERUSALEM ARTICHOKES, PEELED WEIGHT
450 G (1 LB) LAMB FILLET, CUT INTO 5 CM (2 IN) CUBES
15 G (½ OZ) BUTTER
1 TEASPOON PLAIN FLOUR

FOR THE MARINADE
½ GARLIC CLOVE, SLICED
1 FRESH RED CHILLI PEPPER, SLICED
4 TABLESPOONS EXTRA VIRGIN OLIVE OIL
1 TEASPOON CHOPPED FRESH MINT
1 TEASPOON CHOPPED FRESH SAGE
1 TEASPOON CHOPPED FRESH ROSEMARY
GRATED RIND ½ LEMON AND JUICE OF 1 LEMON
SEA SALT
FRESHLY GROUND BLACK PEPPER
1 GLASS DRY RED WINE

METHOD

Cut the artichokes into 5 mm (¼ in) slices and simmer gently in plenty of salted water until just *al dente*. Refresh in very cold water. Mix together the marinade ingredients, and add the lamb and cooked artichokes. Leave to marinate for at least 2–3 hours – the longer the better. Thread alternate pieces of lamb and artichoke onto 4 skewers, allowing 8 cubes of lamb for each skewer. Barbecue the skewers to taste.

Meanwhile, melt the butter in a pan, add the flour and cook gently, stirring, for 2 minutes. Gradually stir in the marinade ingredients and slowly bring to the boil. Simmer the sauce for 2–3 minutes and serve with the skewers.

lamb with fennel and marsala
agnello con finocchio al marsala

After visiting the amazing Florio company, one of the oldest producers of Marsala in Sicily, and tasting some of its rare vintages, I appreciated how suitable this strong wine is, not only for making *scaloppine* and zabaglione, but also for partnering with lamb. This dish could be made with rabbit or chicken, too. Leafy wild fennel grows in abundance in Sicily but it can be replaced here with bulb fennel. The combination of flavours is unusual but very good.

SERVES 4

12 BEST END OF NECK LAMB CUTLETS

PLAIN FLOUR FOR DUSTING

OLIVE OIL FOR FRYING

1 GARLIC CLOVE, FINELY CHOPPED

1 FENNEL BULB AND ITS LEAVES, CUT INTO SMALL CHUNKS

1 GLASS OF VINTAGE DRY MARSALA

SALT AND FRESHLY GROUND BLACK PEPPER

METHOD

Dust the lamb cutlets in flour, shaking off any excess. Heat a little olive oil in a large frying pan and fry the cutlets on both sides until brown. Remove from the pan and set aside. Add the garlic and fennel to the pan and fry for a few minutes, stirring. Add the Marsala and some salt and pepper, then return the cutlets to the pan. Cook gently for 15 minutes and then serve.

lamb cutlets with artichokes
braciole d'abbacchio con carciofi

The combination of lamb and artichokes is always associated with Lazio, and particularly with Rome. Here is a very simple but effective recipe. If you are unable to find the very tender, small artichokes used in Rome, then use larger ones, removing the chokes and cutting the hearts into quarters.

SERVES 4

16 SMALL ARTICHOKES

8 LAMB CHOPS

6 TABLESPOONS OLIVE OIL

1 GARLIC CLOVE, FINELY CHOPPED

1 SMALL ONION, FINELY CHOPPED

1 SPRIG OF MARJORAM

2 GLASSES OF DRY WHITE WINE

250 ML (8 FL OZ) CHICKEN STOCK

SALT AND FRESHLY GROUND BLACK PEPPER

METHOD

Cut the top third off each artichoke and discard the tough outer leaves until you reach the tender heart. Peel the stems. Keep the artichoke hearts in acidulated water to prevent discoloration.

Season the chops and fry them in the olive oil (originally lard was used) until browned on both sides. Remove from the pan and set aside. Add the garlic and onion to the pan and fry gently for a few minutes, until softened. Stir in the marjoram sprig, artichokes, wine and stock. Bring to a simmer, then cover the pan and cook for 10 minutes, until the artichokes are tender. Return the chops to the pan and cook gently for 10 minutes on a lower heat. Adjust the seasoning and serve immediately.

stuffed lamb cutlets
costoline di agnello ripiene

This is a derivation of *Cotoletta alla Valdostana* which uses local veal cutlets and Fontina cheese. The advantage of this recipe is that you can prepare it in advance and cook it at the last minute. 'French-trimmed' cutlets can be prepared by your butcher. Most of the fat and other material is removed, leaving just the bone and the round lean meat section at the end.

SERVES 4

16 x 2.5 CM (1 IN) LAMB CUTLETS, FRENCH-TRIMMED

SEA SALT

FRESHLY GROUND BLACK PEPPER

75 G (3 OZ) FONTINA OR GRUYÈRE CHEESE, CUT INTO SLIVERS

16 LARGE FRESH SAGE LEAVES

75 G (3 OZ) PARMA HAM, SLICED

2 EGGS, BEATEN WITH A PINCH OF SEA SALT

300 G (11 OZ) FINE DRIED BREADCRUMBS

OLIVE OIL FOR SHALLOW FRYING

METHOD

Cut down the centre of the meat of each cutlet until almost through and open out. Season with salt and pepper, then place a sliver of Fontina or Gruyère cheese on one side followed by a sage leaf and a little Parma ham. Fold over the other side of the meat. Dip the cutlets in egg and breadcrumbs to completely coat the meat. Press the cutlets together to seal and slightly flatten the meat. Shallow fry in moderately hot oil until golden on both sides.

Serve 4 cutlets per person.

veal escalopes with marsala
scaloppine al marsala secco

I cooked this in Calatafimi, the Sicilian town where Garibaldi's victory helped initiate the unification of Italy in 1860. An appropriate dish for such an historic spot, it combines veal, popular in the North, with Marsala, the pride of Sicily. Escalopes of chicken or turkey, or even fish such as monkfish or John Dory, can be substituted for the veal.

SERVES 4

500 G (1 LB 2 OZ) VEAL ESCALOPES, CUT 5 MM (¼ IN) THICK

PLAIN FLOUR FOR DUSTING

6 TABLESPOONS EXTRA VIRGIN OLIVE OIL OR 50 G (2 OZ) BUTTER

1 GLASS OF VINTAGE DRY MARSALA

SALT AND FRESHLY GROUND BLACK PEPPER

METHOD

Dust the escalopes in flour on both sides, shaking off any excess. Heat the oil or butter in a large, heavy frying pan. Fry the veal for a couple of minutes on each side, cooking it in batches so as not to overcrowd the pan. When all the escalopes are done, put them all back in the pan and add the wine and some seasoning. Stir for a few seconds; the meat should become lightly glazed because of the combination of flour and wine. Serve immediately.

braised beef in nebbiolo wine
brasato al nebbiolo

The Nebbiolo grape is the father and mother of Barolo and is also used for making many other Piemontese wines, like Carema. Piemontese beef is particularly tasty. The union with Nebbiolo wine brings out the best in it and, after 2 hours cooking, it is tender and juicy. The alcohol evaporates during the cooking so you won't get tipsy when eating this robust but very tasty dish!

SERVES 4

2 MEDIUM-SIZED ONIONS

2 CARROTS

3 STICKS CELERY

1 KG (2¼ LB) BEEF TOPSIDE

2 SPRIGS ROSEMARY

100 G (4 OZ) BUTTER

5 TABLESPOONS OLIVE OIL

5 SAGE LEAVES

2 GARLIC CLOVES

1 LITRE (1¾ PINTS) NEBBIOLO WINE

500 ML (18 FL OZ) STOCK

SALT AND FRESHLY GROUND BLACK PEPPER

METHOD

Chop the onions, carrots and celery into small cubes and put to one side.

With a knife, slightly flatten the piece of meat to make it easier to roll. Place the rosemary inside, roll and bind with string. Season the joint all over with salt and pepper.

Heat the butter and oil in a large pan. Add the meat and seal very well until brown all over. Then add the chopped vegetables and fry until golden. Add the sage leaves and chopped garlic. When the vegetables have turned a nice colour, add the wine and the stock.

Cover with a lid and simmer for 1¾ hours. Take out and place on a serving dish with the sauce and vegetables.

luganiga sausage in red wine
luganiga al vino rosso

This is what I prepared for the fashion students of the Carlo Secoli Institute in Milan on the day of their end-of-year exams. It was a welcome break on a very tense day. They devoured everything within 10 minutes! *Luganiga* is an 'endless' pork sausage which you can buy by the metre in Italy. You can use 100% pork sausage, if you can get it, instead. In the winter, *luganiga* can be served cooked in a tomato sauce with polenta.

SERVES 4

675 G (1½ LB) *LUGANIGA* SAUSAGE

2 TABLESPOONS OLIVE OIL

3 TABLESPOONS RED WINE

2 SPRIGS ROSEMARY

2 TABLESPOONS STOCK

METHOD

Take the sausage and coil it tightly into a spiral. Fix some long cocktail sticks through the diameter of the sausage so that it is held solid and can be turned without breaking. Make the spiral as large as your frying pan.

Heat the oil in the frying pan and fry the sausage for 5 minutes on a high heat on one side. Then turn it over, lower the flame and cook for another 5 minutes. Add the wine, which will give a lovely flavour to the sausage, and place the rosemary sprigs in between the rings. Cook until the wine evaporates, another 5–6 minutes, ensuring both sides are golden brown.

Remove the sausage and place on a preheated serving plate. Keep the pan on the heat, deglaze with the stock and pour this over the sausage.

medallions of beef with mushrooms
medagliono di manzo con funghi

You can use both types of chanterelles, winter or summer, or fresh morels instead of the hedgehog mushrooms (*Hydnum repandum*). Always check a reliable reference book before picking wild mushrooms.

SERVES 4

1 LARGE ONION, FINELY CHOPPED

1 GARLIC CLOVE, FINELY CHOPPED

CHOPPED FRESH RED CHILLI PEPPER TO TASTE

65 G (2½ OZ) BUTTER

1 TABLESPOON CHOPPED FRESH BASIL

2 TABLESPOONS CHOPPED FRESH CHIVES

1 TABLESPOON CHOPPED FRESH SAGE

400 G (14 OZ) FRESH HEDGEHOG MUSHROOMS, CLEANED AND SLICED

SEA SALT

120 ML (4 FL OZ) BEEF STOCK, OR A BOUILLON CUBE

2 TABLESPOONS EXTRA VIRGIN OLIVE OIL

12 x 50 G (2 OZ) MEDALLIONS OF BEEF, TAKEN FROM THE SMALLER
   END OF THE FILLET

METHOD

Fry the onion, garlic and chilli gently in the butter until soft without colouring. Stir in the basil, chives and sage, cooking gently for 1 minute, then stir in the mushrooms and a little salt to extract the juices. When this happens, add the stock and fry for 1–2 minutes until the mushrooms are cooked but still *al dente*.

In another pan, heat the olive oil. When very hot, add the medallions of beef and brown quickly on both sides. Then the cooking time is up to you, depending on how well done you like your meat.

Transfer the medallions to warmed plates and spoon over the sauce. Serve with sautéd potatoes.

calf's liver with marsala
fegato al marsala

The Southern counterpart of *Fegato alla Veneziana* is this liver dish, which promises all the flavours of the South. For a traditional meal, serve with fried potatoes and lightly cooked spinach.

SERVES 4

400 G (14 OZ) CALF'S LIVER, SLICED INTO THIN STRIPS

2 TABLESPOONS PLAIN FLOUR

4 TABLESPOONS OLIVE OIL

6 SAGE LEAVES, FINELY CHOPPED

2 TABLESPOONS FINELY CHOPPED FRESH PARSLEY

120 ML (4 FL OZ) DRY MARSALA

SALT AND FRESHLY GROUND BLACK PEPPER

METHOD

Dust the pieces of liver in the flour, shaking off any excess. Heat the oil in a large, heavy frying pan, add the liver and fry on each side for 1–2 minutes; it's important not to overcook it. Cook in batches if necessary so as not to overcrowd the pan.

Add the sage, parsley and some salt and pepper. Pour in the Marsala and stir to coat all the pieces of liver, which will become shiny and glazed. Remove from the heat and serve immediately.

graziella's chicken

pollo di graziella

Graziella is one of the few self-taught female chefs at the head of a five-star restaurant kitchen in Italy. She learned her trade in her mother's kitchen, which was probably full of recipes from previous mothers. Graziella prepares genuine Pugliese food at Masseria San Domenico, a five-star hotel in Savelletri, where it is a rare pleasure to eat regional specialities, mostly based on the excellent local vegetables, rather than the bland international food often served in hotels. This chicken dish should ideally be cooked in a terracotta pot placed in a wood-fired oven in a sandwich of glowing coals. However, it is also excellent cooked slowly in a conventional oven at home.

SERVES 6

1 x 2 KG (4½ LB) FREE-RANGE CHICKEN, CUT INTO CHUNKS
(INCLUDING THE GIBLETS)

3 GARLIC CLOVES, CHOPPED

2 TABLESPOONS CHOPPED FRESH PARSLEY

5 BAY LEAVES

2 SPRIGS OF ROSEMARY

2 GLASSES OF DRY WHITE WINE

1 GLASS OF EXTRA VIRGIN OLIVE OIL

1 KG (2¼ LB) POTATOES, PEELED AND QUARTERED

3 TABLESPOONS FRESHLY GRATED PARMESAN OR PECORINO CHEESE

SALT AND FRESHLY GROUND BLACK PEPPER

METHOD

Preheat the oven to 190°C/375°F/Gas Mark 5.

The method is quite simple. Mix all the ingredients together in a terracotta pot, cover with a lid and leave to marinate for 1 hour. Place in the oven and cook for at least 1½ hours, or until everything is tender and succulent.

chicken scaloppine with herbs
scaloppine di pollo con erbe

The combination of poached meat and herbs makes a very delicious dish for the summer which isn't too heavy. As in many other cases where pale meat is used, more fantasy is required in your use of herbs and flavouring to give a tasty result. If you cut the breast in strips from where it meets the bone in the shape of an octopus the greater surface area means more flavour can be absorbed – and the cooking time is reduced.

SERVES 4

4 SKINLESS CHICKEN BREASTS, WITH THE BONE

2 TABLESPOONS SEASONED PLAIN FLOUR

75 G (3 OZ) UNSALTED BUTTER

1 TABLESPOON EXTRA VIRGIN OLIVE OIL

1 TABLESPOON EACH OF THE FOLLOWING FINELY CHOPPED FRESH HERBS:
  CHERVIL, DILL, PARSLEY, CHIVES, BASIL, MINT AND ROSEMARY

½ GARLIC CLOVE, FINELY CHOPPED

¼ FRESH RED CHILLI PEPPER, FINELY CHOPPED, OR TO TASTE

GRATED RIND AND JUICE OF 1 LIME

4 TABLESPOONS CHICKEN STOCK

4 TABLESPOONS DRY WHITE WINE

SEA SALT

METHOD

Dust each chicken breast with the seasoned flour and fry over a moderate heat in half the butter and the oil to brown on both sides. Keep warm.

In the same pan, melt the remaining butter. Add the herbs, garlic, chilli and the rind and juice of the lime, stock and white wine. Return the chicken to the pan and poach for about 10 minutes until it is cooked. Season with salt and serve with the sauce.

jewish chicken rissoles

ngozzamoddi or *azmot*

Many Roman dishes are borrowed from the local Jewish community. Although strict Jews have to follow at least 55 dietary rules, I didn't feel at all restricted by the two dishes I borrowed from Donatella Limentani Pavoncello, a Roman lady, a conscientious follower of her religion, and an excellent cook and cookery writer. This recipe has been in her family for 400 years and particularly appealed to me for its simplicity. Donatella traditionally adds a couple of wishbones to the sauce for good luck.

SERVES 4

600 G (1 LB 5 OZ) SKINLESS, BONELESS CHICKEN BREASTS

2 EGGS, BEATEN

4 TABLESPOONS FRESH BREADCUMBS

A PINCH OF CINNAMON

6 TABLESPOONS OLIVE OIL

2 CELERY STICKS, CUT INTO SMALL CUBES

1 GARLIC CLOVE, FINELY CHOPPED

600 G (1 LB 5 OZ) *POLPA DI POMODORO* (TOMATO PULP)

A LITTLE STOCK OR WATER, IF NECESSARY

SALT AND FRESHLY GROUND BLACK PEPPER

METHOD

Roughly mince the chicken. Put it in a bowl and mix together with the eggs, breadcrumbs, cinnamon and some salt and pepper. Use your hands to shape the mixture into 12 rissoles.

Heat the oil in a large frying pan, add the rissoles and fry for 2–3 minutes on each side, until brown. Remove from the pan and set aside. Add the celery, garlic and tomato pulp to the pan, bring to the boil and simmer for 5 minutes. Return the rissoles to the pan and cook for another 10 minutes, adding a little stock or water if the sauce thickens too much. Serve with bread.

roast goose

oca arrosto

I know, I know: fat! We live in an age when fat is almost banned but, all the same, in my opinion the fact that a roasted goose produces a fifth of its weight in pure melted fat which you can use for producing other wonderful food is a bonus. The rest of the meat, when cooked properly, is a delicacy reminiscent of bygone times. I have included this recipe here in case you are lucky enough to get hold of a good goose and you want to know how to deal with it. There is a cabbage dish that is really fantastic with goose – *Cavolo Rosso con Mele* (page 119). You could also serve it with *Peperoni al Balsamico* (page 112). These dishes taste even better eaten three days after cooking. (Remember to multiply the quantities of these recipes by 2½ to feed 10.)

SERVES 10

4.5 KG (10 LB) FRESH GOOSE, OVEN-READY WEIGHT

2 TABLESPOONS EXTRA VIRGIN OLIVE OIL

SEA SALT

FRESHLY GROUND BLACK PEPPER

150 ML (5 FL OZ) WATER

METHOD

Preheat the oven to 190°C/375°F/Gas Mark 5.

Place the goose in a large roasting pan, breast up, and rub the oil into the skin. Season with salt and pepper inside and out. Pour the water into the pan, cover with foil, sealing round the edges, and roast the goose for 2 hours. Remove from the oven and baste with the juices from time to time to encourage a crisp skin. Return to the oven uncovered for a further 30 minutes.

Drain and reserve the fat, ensuring that you have none of the impurities. If necessary, chill the fat. The impurities will sink to the bottom and, after solidifying, the fat can be removed.

Rest the goose for 15 minutes. Remove the breast, carve and serve with the cabbage and pepper dishes as above.

duck verdi-style
anitra alla verdi

I prepared this dish for the first time in Busseto near Parma, birthplace of the great maestro, Giuseppe Verdi, for the finalists in the vocal competition dedicated to him. The delicious simplicity of this dish would certainly meet the approval of one of the greatest composers of all time – at least I hope it would! It perfectly combines the local ingredients, duck and Parma ham.

SERVES 4

1.5 KG (3 LB) DUCK

2 MEDIUM-SIZED CARROTS

1 MEDIUM-SIZED ONION

2 TABLESPOONS OLIVE OIL

150 G (5 OZ) PARMA HAM (MOSTLY FAT WITH LITTLE LEAN),
   MINCED TO A PASTE

SPRIG ROSEMARY

SALT AND FRESHLY GROUND BLACK PEPPER

METHOD

Preheat the oven to 220°C/425°F/Gas Mark 7.

Singe the duck to ensure all the little feathers are burnt off, if necessary. Remove the giblets and season with salt and pepper.

Chop the onion and carrots into small cubes. Scatter into a roasting pan and place the duck on top. Rub the olive oil all over the duck. Take the minced Parma ham fat and spread over the top of the breast and place the sprig of rosemary on top. Cover with foil and place in the oven. After 1 hour remove the foil and roast for a further 15 minutes so that the duck becomes crispy.

If desired, you can serve the duck with the vegetables cooked with it. However, you should avoid the oil and fat left on the bottom of the pan. This is delicious with *Peperoni al Balsamico* (see page 112).

sardinian-style partridge
pernice alla sarda

In honour of the Sardinian hunting tradition, here is a recipe for a noble bird which will surprise many game lovers. Chicken, other small birds and even eel are prepared in the same way.

SERVES 4

8 PARTRIDGES, CLEANED

120 ML (4 FL OZ) EXTRA VIRGIN OLIVE OIL

4 TABLESPOONS WHITE WINE VINEGAR

3 TABLESPOONS FINELY CHOPPED FRESH PARSLEY

1 TABLESPOON SALTED CAPERS, SOAKED IN WATER FOR 10 MINUTES, THEN DRAINED AND FINELY CHOPPED

SALT

METHOD

Simmer the partridges in a large pan of lightly salted water for 20 minutes. Drain the birds and cut them into quarters. Mix together the oil, vinegar, parsley, capers and some salt. Pour this mixture over the birds, cover and leave to marinate for 24 hours. Serve cold.

4 fish

angry red mullet triglie incazzate ▪ baked shellfish frutti di mare gratinati ▪ fish broth brodetto di pesce ▪ swordfish rolls involtini di pesce spada ▪ sea bass with herbs branzino alle erbe ▪ monkfish conte carlo coda di rospo alla conte carlo ▪ baked tuna with herbs tonno al forno con salmoriglio ▪ tuna ragù ragù di tonno ▪ charcoal-grilled sea bass branzino alla brace ▪ trout in a bag trota in cartoccio ▪ baked lobster aragosta al forno ▪ baked sole with parmesan sogliole gratinate ▪ turbot with honey fungus and judas ears rombo con chiodini e orecchie di juda ▪ baked fillets of lake bream lavarelli in teglia ▪ marinated fried sardines sarde alla scapece ▪ mixed fried fish burano-style fritto misto di burano ▪ swordfish with tomato sauce pesce spada agghiotta

angry red mullet
triglie incazzate

'*Incazzate*', like '*arrabbiate*', means literally 'angry' but in cookery has come to mean hot due to the addition of chilli.

SERVES 4

75 G (3 OZ) BUTTER

1 TABLESPOON FINELY CHOPPED SAGE

1 TABLESPOON FINELY CHOPPED ROSEMARY

1 TABLESPOON FINELY CHOPPED PARSLEY

1 TABLESPOON COARSELY CHOPPED FRESH CHILLI PEPPER

4 RED MULLET, 250 G (9 OZ) EACH, SCALED AND FILLETED

1 GLASS RED WINE

SALT

SPRIG OF ROSEMARY, TO DECORATE

METHOD

Heat the butter in a pan, add the herbs and chilli and stir-fry for half a minute. Add the fillets of fish and fry for 1–2 minutes on each side. Set aside the fish and deglaze the pan with the wine. Taste for salt. Reunite the fish with the sauce, warm and serve decorated with a sprig of rosemary.

baked shellfish
frutti di mare gratinati

Frutti di mare are fully appreciated in the Mediterranean because they can be eaten fresh from the sea and raw with the help of a little lemon juice. Every seaside resort in Italy has its own speciality based on *frutti di mare* either raw, baked or grilled. One of the most delightful ways to eat shellfish is as described below, just sprinkled with good olive oil, parsley, garlic, breadcrumbs and a little salt. You can use all sorts of shellfish for this.

SERVES 4

8 SMALL QUEEN SCALLOPS

4 OYSTERS (OPTIONAL)

24 LARGE MUSSELS

8 RAZOR SHELLS

8 CLAMS

8 TABLESPOONS EXTRA VIRGIN OLIVE OIL

1 GARLIC CLOVE FIRST CRUSHED, THEN VERY FINELY CHOPPED

4 TABLESPOONS DRIED FINE BREADCRUMBS

2 TABLESPOONS FINELY CHOPPED FRESH FLAT-LEAF PARSLEY

SEA SALT

FRESHLY GROUND BLACK PEPPER

LEMON WEDGES

METHOD

Preheat the oven to 240°C/475°F/Gas Mark 9.

First prepare the shellfish. Detach the scallops and oysters carefully from their shells and separate the coral from the white flesh of the scallop. Put the mussels, razor shells and clams in a pan, cover and place over a high heat for 1–2 minutes until the shells open. Remove the top shell of each mussel, discarding any that do not open. Mix the oil and chopped garlic.

Arrange each shell, with its own meat inside, on an ovenproof dish. Sprinkle with breadcrumbs, parsley, salt and pepper and sprinkle the garlic and oil on top. Bake for 10–15 minutes until brown. Serve hot, garnished with lemon wedges, but they are also delicious cold.

fish broth

brodetto di pesce

Brodetto is the diminutive of *brodo* and means literally 'small broth'. Although it is usually made with meat or chicken, here I use fish stock. You can buy this from good supermarkets or easily make it at home by asking the fishmonger for tasty bits and pieces. The fishmonger will also be able to help you with the choice of fish because it will all depend on the catch of the day. This dish is wonderful eaten with the croûtons of garlic bread called *fettunta*. Make these by toasting slices of bread and gently rubbing a garlic clove over them, and then brush with a little extra virgin olive oil.

SERVES 4

36 LARGE MUSSELS, TIGHTLY CLOSED

8 RAW KING PRAWNS

200 G (7 OZ) MONKFISH

8 TABLESPOONS EXTRA VIRGIN OLIVE OIL

½ GARLIC CLOVE, CRUSHED

¼ FRESH RED CHILLI PEPPER, CHOPPED, OR TO TASTE

100 G (4 OZ) FENNEL OR FENNEL TOPS

1 LARGE TOMATO, COARSELY CHOPPED

750 ML (1¼ PINTS) FISH STOCK

GRATED RIND 1 LEMON

8 ANCHOVY FILLETS

SEA SALT

FRESHLY GROUND BLACK PEPPER

METHOD

Scrub the mussels under cold running water and, with a small sharp knife, scrape away the beard. Wash in several changes of cold water until the water is left clean. Peel the prawns. Remove all membrane from the monkfish and cut into 5 cm (2 in) pieces.

Heat the oil and fry the garlic and chilli for 15 seconds only. Add the fennel and tomato and cook for 2 minutes, then add the stock, lemon rind and the fish and shellfish. Simmer for 10 minutes until all the shellfish are open and cooked. Check the seasoning and serve.

swordfish rolls

involtini di pesce spada

No one knows who invented this recipe, although both Sicilians and Calabrians claim the rights to it. It doesn't matter to us; we can just enjoy this simple dish.

SERVES 4

75 G (3 OZ) STALE BREAD

6 TABLESPOONS OLIVE OIL

25 G (1 OZ) PARMESAN CHEESE, CUT INTO VERY SMALL CUBES

50 G (2 OZ) PROVOLA CHEESE, CUT INTO VERY SMALL CUBES

1 TABLESPOON SALTED CAPERS, SOAKED IN WATER FOR 10 MINUTES, THEN DRAINED AND FINELY CHOPPED

2 TABLESPOONS CHOPPED FRESH PARSLEY

8 SLICES OF SWORDFISH (PREFERABLY CUT FROM THE BELLY), ABOUT 5 MM (¼ IN) THICK

15 G (½ OZ) BUTTER, CUT INTO 8 SMALL STRIPS

JUICE OF 1 LEMON

SALT AND FRESHLY GROUND BLACK PEPPER

METHOD

To make the filling, crumble the bread into a bowl, add 1 tablespoon of the oil and 1 tablespoon of water and mix together with your hands to loosen the bread. Then add the cheeses, capers, half the parsley and some salt and pepper. Mix together to form a soft dough.

Put the swordfish slices on a work surface and place a piece of the filling rolled into a sausage shape on top of each one. Place a strip of butter on the filling and roll up the fish. Secure with wooden cocktail sticks.

Heat the remaining oil in a large pan and fry the rolls for 2 minutes on each side. Sprinkle with the lemon juice and the remaining parsley and serve with some of the cooking juices poured over.

sea bass with herbs
branzino alle erbe

The Italians prefer sea bass to any other fish. They call it *spigola* or *branzino*. It is white with firm meat which keeps a fantastic taste of the sea. Here, it is cooked in foil and when you open the parcel a wonderful aroma is released. Serve it with freshly boiled new potatoes and green beans sautéd in a little butter. Remember to collect the juices and herbs and spoon them over each serving. When you buy a *spigola* make sure that it is very fresh, with clear eyes, very red gills and your fishmonger's guarantee that it is really fresh. You should never cook this dish with a frozen fish. However, feel free to choose your own preferred fish (such as grey mullet) should you not find sea bass.

SERVES 4

1 x 1.75 KG (4 LB) SEA BASS, CLEANED, SCALED AND FINS REMOVED

1 LEMON, CUT INTO 7 SLICES

2 SPRIGS FRESH THYME

6 TABLESPOONS EXTRA VIRGIN OLIVE OIL

1 TABLESPOON FINELY CHOPPED FRESH MINT

2 STALKS FRESH FLAT-LEAF PARSLEY, FINELY CHOPPED

1 TABLESPOON FINELY CHOPPED FRESH FENNEL LEAVES (OPTIONAL)

20 LEAVES FRESH BASIL, FINELY CHOPPED

1 BUNCH FRESH CHIVES, FINELY CHOPPED

1 TABLESPOON CELERY LEAVES, FINELY CHOPPED

JUICE ½ LEMON

SEA SALT

FRESHLY GROUND BLACK PEPPER

METHOD

Preheat the oven to 200°C/400°F/Gas Mark 6.

Dry the sea bass thoroughly with kitchen paper. Take a large piece of foil and place it in an ovenproof dish. Put the lemon slices onto it and place the fish on top. Season the inside of the fish, adding the sprigs of thyme. Using your hands, massage 4 tablespoons of the oil into the skin of the fish and season with salt and pepper.

Mix the mint, parsley, fennel leaves, basil, chives and celery leaves. Place half the herbs inside the fish. Bring up the sides of the foil to enclose the fish and seal the edges carefully – you will need to open and seal the foil again at a later stage. Bake for 30 minutes.

Remove from the oven and carefully open the foil. Mix the remaining herbs with the lemon juice and remaining 2 tablespoons of oil and spoon over the top of the fish. Leave the foil open but gathered round the fish to protect it from the fierce heat of the oven and bake for a further 5 minutes. Make sure the fish is cooked by piercing the flesh by the backbone.

To serve the fish, make an incision along its back, detach the fillet from the head and tail and remove completely from the fish. Cut each fillet in two. Turn over and repeat. Spoon over the herbs and juices and serve.

monkfish conte carlo
coda di rospo alla conte carlo

A cooking Count is not the kind of person you meet every day. Conte Carlo Maria Rocca from Venice is one of the most charming gourmet cooks I have ever encountered. It was delightful to shop with him at the Rialto market where he was well known and where he showed great talent in spotting the best ingredients. After an *ombra*, a glass of wine, in *Bacchero*, a typical Venetian wine bar, I sampled real Venetian food. The Count is a great entertainer and he created this simple and delicious dish. Monkfish can be replaced with John Dory, turbot or halibut, so long as the fish is boneless. Slice the potatoes to about 1 mm thick – use a mandolin or food processor for best results.

SERVES 6

2 KG (4½ LB) WAXY POTATOES, PEELED AND VERY THINLY SLICED

20 SAGE LEAVES

ABUNDANT EXTRA VIRGIN OLIVE OIL

1.5 KG (3 LB) MONKFISH, CUT INTO FLAT FILLETS

100 G (4 OZ) FRESHLY GRATED PARMESAN

SALT AND FRESHLY GROUND PEPPER TO TASTE

METHOD

Preheat the oven to 200°C/400°F/Gas Mark 6.

Arrange half the thinly sliced potatoes in a thin layer in a large ovenproof dish with half the sage. Sprinkle with some oil, cover with the fillets and sprinkle with half of the Parmesan. Cover with another layer of potato slices, sprinkle with some more oil, add the rest of the sage leaves and the remaining Parmesan, salt and pepper. Bake in the oven for about 1 hour until the potatoes are tender.

baked tuna with herbs
tonno al forno con salmoriglio

It is a joy to shop in the Vucceria market of Palermo. The fish is so fresh and so appetizingly displayed that it is impossible to resist. Fresh tuna is now available everywhere, often replacing meat because it does not have a noticeably fishy taste. For this recipe you could substitute swordfish or any large fish that can be cut into thick slices. Tuna, however, is perfect, and the aristocratic guests I cooked it for in Palermo were most enthusiastic about my interpretation of Sicilian cooking. They were intrigued to see that the *salmoriglio*, a mixture of herbs generally used to dress steamed or grilled fish, was cooked with the fish in this case.

SERVES 4

4 x 200 G (7 OZ) FRESH TUNA STEAKS

2 TABLESPOONS PINE KERNELS

2 TABLESPOONS DRIED BREADCRUMBS

FOR THE *SALMORIGLIO*

4 GARLIC CLOVES, CHOPPED

3 TABLESPOONS VERY FINELY CHOPPED FRESH MINT

3 TABLESPOONS VERY FINELY CHOPPED FRESH PARSLEY

2 TABLESPOONS SALTED CAPERS, SOAKED IN WATER FOR 10 MINUTES, THEN DRAINED

JUICE AND GRATED RIND OF 2 LEMONS

1 TEASPOON DRIED WILD OREGANO

EXTRA VIRGIN OLIVE OIL

SALT AND FRESHLY GROUND BLACK PEPPER

METHOD

Preheat the oven to 220°C/425°F/Gas Mark 7.

To make the *salmoriglio*, put the chopped garlic in a mortar and pound it to a fine pulp. Add the mint, parsley, capers, lemon juice and rind, oregano and enough olive oil to make an almost liquid mixture. Pound together to make a thick sauce, then season with salt and pepper.

Season the tuna steaks, place them on an oiled baking tray and spread the *salmoriglio* over them. Sprinkle the breadcrumbs and pine kernels on top and bake for 6–7 minutes, until the tuna is just cooked through.

tuna ragù

ragù di tonno

This recipe is from Sicily, where tuna is cooked in many different ways. You can serve it with pasta, tossing the pasta with the tomato sauce and then eating the tuna afterwards as a main course. The tuna can also be eaten cold, which makes it easier to slice.

SERVES 6

A NICE PIECE OF FRESH TUNA, WEIGHING 1.25 KG (2½ LB)

3 GARLIC CLOVES, CUT INTO SLIVERS

A FEW SPRIGS OF MINT

6 TABLESPOONS OLIVE OIL

1 ONION, FINELY SLICED

4 ANCHOVY FILLETS, CHOPPED

1 TABLESPOON SALTED CAPERS, SOAKED IN WATER FOR 10 MINUTES,
   THEN DRAINED

1 KG (2½ LB) *POLPA DI POMODORO* (TOMATO PULP)

SALT AND FRESHLY GROUND BLACK PEPPER

METHOD

With a small, sharp knife, make a few incisions in the tuna and insert the garlic slivers and sprigs of mint. Tie with string to keep the tuna in shape.

Heat the olive oil in a large pan and fry the tuna on a high heat just until browned on both sides. Reduce the heat, add the onion and fry until soft, then add the anchovy fillets and capers. Stir in the tomato pulp and cook gently for 20–30 minutes, until the tomatoes have formed a sauce and the fish is cooked through. Season to taste, then remove the piece of tuna, cut off the string and slice the fish. Serve with the sauce.

charcoal-grilled sea bass
branzino alla brace

In Sardinia this recipe is made with various types of scaly fish. The marinade and the scales help the flesh remain juicy and flavoursome during grilling. Originally the marinade was made with seawater, but because it is difficult to find completely clean and unpolluted, it is better to use water in which you have dissolved some sea salt.

SERVES 4

4 x 450 G (1 LB) SEA BASS, CLEANED BUT NOT SCALED

EXTRA VIRGIN OLIVE OIL, FOR FRYING

FRESHLY GROUND BLACK PEPPER (OPTIONAL)

FOR THE MARINADE

300 ML (10 FL OZ) WATER

50 G (2 OZ) SEA SALT

JUICE OF 1 LEMON

2 TABLESPOONS WHITE WINE VINEGAR

2 TABLESPOONS VERY FINELY CHOPPED FRESH CHIVES

METHOD

To make the marinade, put the water and salt in a pan and boil until the salt has dissolved. Leave to cool and then add the lemon juice, vinegar and chives.

Put the fish in a dish, pour over the marinade and leave for 1 hour. Cook the fish on a charcoal grill for 10–12 minutes on each side, basting from time to time with the marinade. Skin and bone the fish, then serve with a drizzle of olive oil and a sprinkling of black pepper, if desired. A very delicate fish indeed.

trout in a bag

trota in cartoccio

Enveloping a fish in a leaf, clay or salt is a method that was used by the ancient Romans. This form of cooking retains the juices in the envelope, enabling the food to be gently cooked in hot moisture and filling it with flavour. You may use either greaseproof paper or aluminium foil, taking care not to envelope the fish too tightly or it will come into contact with the paper which would remove the skin when you open the parcel. The best effect is achieved when the parcel is opened in front of the guests so they can inhale the wonderful aroma.

SERVES 4

4 x 300 G (11 OZ) TROUT

200 G (7 OZ) FENNEL

1 LARGE LEMON

4 SPRIGS PARSLEY

65 G (2½ OZ) BUTTER

SALT AND FRESHLY GROUND BLACK PEPPER

METHOD

Preheat the oven to 200°C/400°F/Gas Mark 6.

Clean, gut and scale the trout or ask the fishmonger to do it. Chop the fennel and slice the lemon very finely.

Scatter the chopped fennel and a few lemon slices in the middle of 4 sheets of greaseproof paper. Season the fish with salt and pepper and place on the fennel. Place a couple of lemon slices inside the fish with a sprig of parsley. Place the remaining lemon slices over the fish and dot with butter.

Seal the edges of the paper making a parcel, place on a baking tray and cook for 20 mintues.

Serve on a long plate opening the parcels in front of your guests.

baked lobster
aragosta al forno

When you have a relative abundance of lobsters and you want to enjoy them prepared simply, as fishermen do in Sardinia, then you don't need to look for sophisticated ways of cooking the king of crustacea.

SERVES 4

4 x 500 G (1 LB 2 OZ) LIVE LOBSTERS

6 TABLESPOONS VIRGIN OLIVE OIL

4 TABLESPOONS VERY FINELY CHOPPED FRESH PARSLEY

JUICE OF 1 LEMON

SALT AND FRESHLY GROUND BLACK PEPPER

METHOD

Preheat the oven to 200°C/400°F/Gas Mark 6.

Cut the live lobsters in half. (If you pierce through the cross mark in the centre of the head they will be killed instantly.) Mix the other ingredients together and pour them over the lobster flesh. Bake for 20–25 minutes, then serve with more lemon juice if desired. It's as simple as that!

baked sole with parmesan
sogliole gratinate

Any dish baked in the oven comes as a relief to those who do not like standing over a hot stove. The only work involved in this recipe is the easy preparation of the fish. The result, as is often the case with simple dishes made from good-quality ingredients, is stunning. The combination of herbs and cheese with fish is very interesting.

SERVES 4

4 x 300 G (11 OZ) DOVER SOLE, CLEANED, SKINNED AND FINS TRIMMED

8 TABLESPOONS DRIED BREADCRUMBS

1 GARLIC CLOVE, VERY FINELY CHOPPED

4 TABLESPOONS FINELY CHOPPED FRESH PARSLEY

6 TABLESPOONS GRATED PECORINO CHEESE

6 TABLESPOONS OLIVE OIL

SALT AND FRESHLY GROUND BLACK PEPPER

METHOD

Preheat the oven to 220°C/425°F/Gas Mark 7.

With a very sharp knife, make an incision right down the centre of each fish to reach the bone. Season the fish with salt and pepper and put them on a baking sheet. Mix the dried breadcrumbs with the garlic and parsley and spread on both sides of the incision, using a spatula. Sprinkle the cheese down the centre, then drizzle the olive oil all over the fish. Bake in the oven for 15 minutes, until the fish are tender.

turbot with honey fungus and judas ears
rombo con chiodini e orecchie di juda

I put this recipe on the menu of my restaurant years ago and it is still one of the favourites. Of course, you have to have the best and freshest of ingredients. You can also make this with other *funghi*, such as horn of plenty and bay boletus, and the result is still spectacular. If these too are unavailable, use cultivated shiitake and oyster mushrooms. If you do collect your own mushrooms, check a reference book first. You can find Judas Ears in Chinese shops where they are also called black or Wood Ear fungus and you can reconstitute them in water. Take care when you fry the Judas Ears because they can explode in fat. If you can't get turbot, use halibut or monkfish instead.

SERVES 4

5 G (⅛ OZ) DRIED PORCINI MUSHROOMS, SOAKED FOR 30 MINUTES
  IN 150 ML (5 FL OZ) TEPID WATER
100 G (4 OZ) HONEY FUNGUS
4 TABLESPOONS EXTRA VIRGIN OLIVE OIL
200 G (7 OZ) JUDAS EAR MUSHROOMS
1 GARLIC CLOVE, CRUSHED
1 TABLESPOON FINELY CHOPPED FRESH FLAT-LEAF PARSLEY
SEA SALT
FRESHLY GROUND BLACK PEPPER
4 x 175 G (6 OZ) FILLETS OF TURBOT

METHOD

Soak the dried mushrooms in tepid water for 30 minutes and squeeze dry, reserving the soaking liquor. If the honey fungus is fresh, boil it in salted water for 10 minutes before sautéing in half the oil.

Fry the Judas Ears gently in the remaining oil with the garlic until they start to crackle in the pan. Remove from the heat and stir in the parsley and honey fungus. Squeeze the porcini dry, chop and add them to the pan along with the soaking liquor. Season to taste with salt and pepper.

Meanwhile, in a separate pan, seal the fish fillets on both sides in hot olive oil. Tip in the contents of the other pan. Fry for 2 more minutes and serve.

baked fillets of lake bream
lavarelli in teglia

This is a delicate and tasty way of cooking lake or river fish. *Lavarelli* and *coregoni* are fished regularly on Lake Maggiore and this is one of the best ways to eat them. In a similar way you can use fillets of other fish with wonderful results.

SERVES 4

4 x 300 G (11 OZ) FILLETS LAKE BREAM

PLAIN WHITE FLOUR FOR DUSTING

120 G (4½ OZ) BUTTER

8 SAGE LEAVES

SALT AND FRESHLY GROUND BLACK PEPPER

METHOD

Preheat the oven to 200°C/400°F/Gas Mark 6.

Dust each fillet in flour and lay on a baking dish adding salt and pepper. Meanwhile, put the butter and sage leaves in a pan and fry until foamy. Pour over the fillets of fish and bake in the oven for 7 minutes.

marinated fried sardines

sarde alla scapece

This method of marinating fried fish and serving it cold is popular throughout the South. Many different fish can be used, such as anchovies, mackerel and sardines. It makes an ideal summer *antipasto* or main course.

SERVES 4

1 KG (2¼ LB) FRESH SARDINES, CLEANED

PLAIN FLOUR FOR DUSTING

100 ML (3½ FL OZ) OLIVE OIL, PLUS EXTRA FOR SHALLOW FRYING

1 GARLIC CLOVE, FINELY SLICED

6 TABLESPOONS WHITE WINE VINEGAR

120 ML (4 FL OZ) DRY WHITE WINE

3 TABLESPOONS FINELY CHOPPED FRESH MINT

SALT AND FRESHLY GROUND BLACK PEPPER

METHOD

Dust the sardines in flour, shaking off any excess, then fry them in plenty of hot olive oil until they are crisp and brown. Transfer to a shallow dish.

In a separate pan, heat the 100 ml (3½ fl oz) olive oil and fry the garlic in it very briefly. Add the vinegar, wine and mint, then remove from the heat. While it is still hot, pour this mixture over the fish. Season to taste and leave to marinate for a couple of hours before serving.

mixed fried fish burano-style

fritto misto di burano

On the small and very pretty island of Burano near Venice, once Italy's centre of handmade embroidery, the gondola regatta is quite a prestigious event. The entire village (about 800 people) takes part. While the youngsters row in the race, the others prepare the most delicious *Fritto Misto di Pesce* which is sold to the thousands of people who travel from all over the area. Every coastal region in Italy has its own *Fritto Misto di Pesce*, but only a few have a *laguna* from which they can catch such delicious fish.

SERVES 4

400 G (14 OZ) FRESH EEL, CLEANED WEIGHT, CUT INTO CHUNKS

8 GIANT MEDITERRANEAN PRAWNS, BODY PEELED BUT HEAD
  AND TAIL STILL ATTACHED

150 G (5 OZ) SQUID OR CUTTLEFISH, CLEANED WEIGHT,
  INCLUDING TENTACLES

PLAIN FLOUR AS REQUIRED FOR DUSTING

OLIVE OIL FOR DEEP FRYING

SALT

2 LEMONS

METHOD

Preheat a deep fryer to 190°C/375°F.

Sprinkle all the fish with salt and coat each piece in flour, ensuring each whole piece of fish is covered. Shake off excess flour. Deep fry the fish for 2–3 minutes, starting with the eel, then the squid or cuttlefish, and fry for an additional 2 minutes. Lastly add the prawns and fry for a minute or two. All the pieces of fish should be a golden-brown colour when cooked. Drain on absorbent paper, then serve with lemon halves on preheated plates.

In Burano, they serve this on pieces of old-fashioned butcher's paper, which I find rather amusing.

swordfish with tomato sauce
pesce spada agghiotta

In the charming village of Scilla in the channel of Messina, the fishermen make a living from fishing for swordfish, which, they claim, gather from all over the Mediterranean Sea to mate in the picturesque bay. The unfortunate 'lovers' are often caught in pairs, destined for the pots and pans of local restaurants. A tragic end to delight the palates of many.

SERVES 4

120 ML (4 FL OZ) EXTRA VIRGIN OLIVE OIL

1 SMALL ONION, FINELY CHOPPED

1 TABLESPOON SALTED CAPERS, SOAKED IN WATER FOR 10 MINUTES, THEN DRAINED

2 TABLESPOONS GREEN OLIVES, PITTED AND CHOPPED

4 x 165 G (5½ OZ) SLICES OF SWORDFISH

1 TABLESPOON CHOPPED FRESH PARSLEY

1 TABLESPOON CHOPPED FRESH BASIL

1 SMALL GLASS OF DRY WHITE WINE

600 G (1 LB 5 OZ) TOMATOES, CHOPPED

SALT AND FRESHLY GROUND BLACK PEPPER

METHOD

Heat the oil in a large pan and briefly fry the onion until softened. Add the capers and olives and cook, stirring, for a couple of minutes. Add the swordfish and fry for a few minutes on each side, until browned. Stir in the parsley, basil and some seasoning, then pour in the wine and let it bubble until most of it has evaporated. Add the tomatoes, lower the heat and cook for 10 minutes, until the sauce has thickened. Adjust the seasoning and serve.

5 vegetables & accompaniments

vegetarian timbale timballino vegetariano ▪ **stuffed onions don pippo** cipolle alla don pippo ▪ **truffled mushrooms** funghi trifolati ▪ **chargrilled vegetables** vegetali arrostiti ▪ **potato croquettes with almonds** crocchette alle mandorle ▪ **vegetable caponata** caponata di verdure ▪ **peppers in balsamic vinegar** peperoni al balsamico ▪ **baby onions with balsamic sauce** cipolline al balsamico ▪ **courgettes with tomato and basil** zucchini al pomodoro e basilico ▪ **broad beans and chicory** fave e cicorie ('ncapriata) ▪ **charcoal-grilled wild mushrooms** funghi misti alla brace ▪ **stuffed tomatoes** pomodori ripieni ▪ **red cabbage with apples** cavolo rosso con mele ▪ **baked potatoes calabrese-style** patate in tegame al forno ▪ **rustic pugliese bread** pane casereccio ▪ **focaccia** ▪ **salad of oranges and lemons** insalata di arance e limoni ▪ **peasant-style beans** fagioli alla cafona

vegetarian timbale
timballino vegetariano

The traditions of vegetable cookery in Italy are the result of using regionally grown produce in a way which could replace meat in times when it was scarce and expensive. This recipe includes a basic tomato sauce which you can also use with spaghetti or for topping pizzas. You may increase the quantities of vegetables in this dish and serve it as a main course if you wish. The quantities here make a wonderful starter.

SERVES 4

120 G (4½ OZ) BROCCOLI FLORETS

90 G (3½ OZ) FRENCH BEANS

2 x 200 G (7 OZ) COURGETTES, CUT LENGTHWISE INTO 5 MM (¼ IN) SLICES

1 x 500 G (1 LB 2 OZ) AUBERGINE, CUT LENGTHWISE INTO 5 MM (¼ IN) SLICES

4 TABLESPOONS SEASONED PLAIN FLOUR

4 EGGS, BEATEN

OLIVE OIL FOR SHALLOW FRYING

200 G (7 OZ) FONTINA OR GRUYÈRE CHEESE, CUT INTO 1 CM (½ IN) DICE

100 G (4 OZ) FRESHLY GRATED PARMESAN

FOR THE TOMATO SAUCE

1 MEDIUM ONION, FINELY CHOPPED

6 TABLESPOONS EXTRA VIRGIN OLIVE OIL

1 x 400 G CAN CHOPPED TOMATOES

6 BASIL LEAVES

SEA SALT

FRESHLY GROUND BLACK PEPPER

METHOD

Preheat the oven to 200°C/400°F/Gas Mark 6.

Make the sauce: fry the onion gently in the oil until soft without colouring. Add the tomatoes and simmer gently for 10 minutes. Stir in the basil, and salt and pepper to taste. Set to one side.

Cook the broccoli and French beans in boiling salted water, drain and refresh in cold water. Dry the broccoli florets on kitchen paper and slice. Cut the beans into 7.5 cm (3 in) pieces.

Dust the courgette, aubergine and broccoli slices with the seasoned flour, patting off any excess, dip in beaten egg and shallow fry in 2.5 cm (1 in) of very hot oil until golden brown on both sides. Drain on kitchen paper.

Into an ovenproof dish put 3 tablespoons of tomato sauce, then layers of aubergine, Fontina or Gruyère cheese, tomato sauce, Parmesan, French beans, courgette, broccoli, tomato sauce, Parmesan and then repeat the layers, ending with a layer of tomato sauce and Parmesan.

Bake for approximately 30 minutes until sizzling.

stuffed onions don pippo
cipolle alla don pippo

The red Tropea onion has a mild, sweet flavour and is usually eaten raw in salads. It is grown in Calabria, particularly in the area round the Capo Vaticano, a promontory on which stands the Tropea lighthouse. This recipe is dedicated to Pippo Benedetto, who has been the lighthouse keeper there for 32 years and has become a sort of local legend. When I cooked for him, the look on his face was enough to convince me that he liked this new way of using onions. You can, of course, substitute other types of onion.

SERVES 4

8 LARGE ONIONS, PREFERABLY RED AND SWEET

200 G (7 OZ) FRESH BREADCRUMBS, SOFTENED IN WATER,
   THEN SQUEEZED DRY

1 TABLESPOON FINELY CHOPPED FRESH BASIL

1 TABLESPOON FINELY CHOPPED FRESH PARSLEY

75 G (3 OZ) PECORINO CHEESE, CUT INTO SMALL CUBES

75 G (3 OZ) PECORINO OR PARMESAN CHEESE, GRATED

1 TABLESPOON SALTED CAPERS, SOAKED IN WATER FOR 10 MINUTES,
   THEN DRAINED AND ROUGHLY CHOPPED

2 EGGS, BEATEN

120 ML (4 FL OZ) OLIVE OIL

2 TABLESPOONS DRIED BREADCRUMBS

SALT AND FRESHLY GROUND BLACK PEPPER

METHOD

Preheat the oven to 200°C/400°F/Gas Mark 6.

Peel the onions and cut the top off each one. With a sharp knife, remove the inside of each onion, leaving a shell about 1 cm (½ in) thick.

Mix together the fresh breadcrumbs, basil, parsley, cubed pecorino, grated cheese, capers, eggs and 2 tablespoons of the olive oil. Season with salt and pepper to taste, then stuff the onions with this mixture. Put them in an ovenproof dish, dust with the dried breadcrumbs and drizzle over the remaining olive oil. Bake for 30 minutes, until the onions are tender.

truffled mushrooms
funghi trifolati

Trifolare is a way of cooking in Italy which involves sautéing with the addition of parsley. You may '*trifolare*' courgettes, aubergines or as in this case, *funghi*, wild or cultivated. The word comes from *trifola* (truffle in the Piemontese dialect) and probably when truffles were not as sought-after and expensive as they are today, they were cooked this way. This is a dish that can be eaten by itself, accompanied by bread or served as a side dish to meat or fish. If you are intending to pick your own wild mushrooms, it is essential to consult a reliable reference book first.

SERVES 4

500 G (1 LB 2 OZ) FRESH WILD MUSHROOMS, OR CULTIVATED
   BUTTON MUSHROOMS
6 TABLESPOONS EXTRA VIRGIN OLIVE OIL
1 GARLIC CLOVE, VERY FINELY CHOPPED
SALT AND PEPPER TO TASTE
2 TABLESPOONS FINELY CHOPPED PARSLEY

METHOD

Clean the mushrooms well, discarding all the impurities – try not to wash if possible. Heat the oil in a pan until very hot, but not smoky. Add all the mushrooms and sauté or stir-fry for 10 minutes, until you see the mushrooms reduce in volume. Then add the garlic and sauté for another 10 minutes. Add salt, pepper and parsley and serve.

chargrilled vegetables
vegetali arrostiti

The entire world seems to have been caught up by the grilled vegetable craze, from California to New York, Paris and Rome, perhaps the best example of today's trend for healthy eating. I firmly believe that there is space in this world for any kind of food and I eat this dish because I like it and not because it is fashionable. In fact, I forget all about meat when I eat it. The process of blanching is essential for the root vegetables because if they are not blanched, they will char on the outside by the time the centre is cooked. I like to use *Radicchio di Treviso*, an elongated version of the more familiar radicchio, sold with its root attached. If you can't get it, use ordinary radicchio.

SERVES 4

250 G (9 OZ) FENNEL

120 G (4½ OZ) COURGETTES

150 G (5 OZ) JERUSALEM ARTICHOKES

250 G (9 OZ) AUBERGINE

75 G (3 OZ) RADICCHIO

225 G (8 OZ) RED PEPPER

120 G (4½ OZ) MUSHROOMS (SHIITAKE, OYSTER OR FIELD)

FOR THE MARINADE

6 TABLESPOONS EXTRA VIRGIN OLIVE OIL

½ GARLIC CLOVE, CRUSHED

1 TABLESPOON VERY FINELY CHOPPED FRESH FLAT-LEAF PARSLEY

JUICE ½ LEMON

SEA SALT

1 GARLIC BULB, TO GARNISH

METHOD

Preheat the grill or griddle.

Cut the fennel into 5 mm (¼ in) slices, vertically. Cut the courgettes and aubergine into 5 mm (¼ in) slices lengthwise. Peel the Jerusalem artichokes and cut into 5 mm (¼ in) slices. If using *Radicchio di Treviso*, peel the root and cut in half. Seed the pepper and cut into quarters lengthwise. Trim the mushroom stalks.

Blanch the fennel and artichokes in salted, boiling water for 3 minutes, drain and refresh in plenty of very cold water. Pat dry with kitchen paper.

Mix the marinade ingredients. Using a brush, baste the sliced vegetables and place on the grill or griddle. Brown slowly on both sides. Remove and baste again. Repeat until all the vegetables are cooked. Arrange on a preheated serving dish and decorate with fried, unpeeled garlic cloves.

potato croquettes with almonds
crocchette alle mandorle

An extremely tasty and useful alternative to plain potato croquettes. Serve as an accompaniment to fish or meat.

SERVES 4-6

500 G (1 LB 2 OZ) POTATOES

1 EGG

100 G (4 OZ) PARMESAN CHEESE, FRESHLY GRATED

100 G (4 OZ) BLANCHED ALMONDS, TOASTED AND COARSELY CHOPPED

150 ML (5 FL OZ) OLIVE OIL

SALT AND FRESHLY GROUND BLACK PEPPER

METHOD

Wash the potatoes well but don't peel them. Put them in a pan of water, bring to the boil and simmer until tender. Drain and leave to cool, then peel and mash them. Mix in the egg, Parmesan cheese and some salt and pepper, then shape into croquettes about 7.5 cm (3 in) long and 2.5 cm (1 in) thick.

Spread the chopped almonds out on a plate and roll the potato croquettes in them. Heat the oil in a frying pan and fry the croquettes over a medium heat until golden brown. Serve hot or cold.

vegetable caponata
caponata di verdure

This is an alternative version of the famous Sicilian *Caponata di Melanzane*, which is based on aubergines. Many more vegetables are included here, resulting in an excellent dish.

SERVES 6

150 ML (5 FL OZ) OLIVE OIL

50 G (2 OZ) DRIED BREADCRUMBS

200 G (7 OZ) CAULIFLOWER FLORETS

3 HEADS OF CHICORY, CUT IN HALF

200 G (7 OZ) CELERY STICKS, CUT INTO CHUNKS

200 G (7 OZ) CARDOONS (THE TENDER CENTRE PART ONLY), CUT INTO CHUNKS (OPTIONAL)

300 G (11 OZ) FRESH SPINACH

200 G (7 OZ) CURLY ENDIVE (*FRISÉ*)

2 TABLESPOONS WHITE WINE VINEGAR

1 TABLESPOON SALTED CAPERS, SOAKED IN WATER FOR 10 MINUTES, THEN DRAINED

8 ANCHOVY FILLETS

SALT AND FRESHLY GROUND BLACK PEPPER

METHOD

Heat 2 tablespoons of the olive oil in a small pan, add the breadcrumbs and fry until browned. Remove from the heat and set aside.

Cook all the vegetables separately in a large pan of lightly salted boiling water until just tender, then drain well. Heat the remaining olive oil in a large frying pan (or, better, a wok), add the cooked vegetables and stir-fry them for 1–2 minutes until well mixed. Stir in the vinegar and some seasoning and mix well again. Place on a serving dish and sprinkle over the breadcrumbs and capers, then garnish with the anchovies. Serve warm or cold, as an *antipasto* or a side dish.

peppers in balsamic vinegar
peperoni al balsamico

One of the most famous producers of traditional balsamic vinegar is Signora Giacobazzi of Modena who loves her wooden barrels so much that she treats them as if they were her best friends. A wooden barrel that holds cooked-down unfermented wine must for up to 50 years and turns it into one of the most sublime and precious condiments on earth has to be your best friend! To savour this dish it is not necessary to use a 50-year-old balsamic vinegar – a good quality, younger, more commercial one is fine.

SERVES 4

3 RED PEPPERS

3 YELLOW PEPPERS

6 TABLESPOONS OLIVE OIL

2 GARLIC CLOVES

2 TABLESPOONS BALSAMIC VINEGAR

SALT TO TASTE

METHOD

Cut the peppers in half, discard the seeds and the stem and cut into strips. Put the olive oil in a frying pan with the peppers on a high heat. When the peppers begin to sizzle loudly, turn them from time to time with a wooden spoon and repeat this to avoid them burning on either side. When the edges begin to brown, add the garlic, which needs to be cooked for a few minutes. Still on a high heat, add the salt and balsamic vinegar. Stir to evaporate the vinegar.

This dish goes well with *Anitra alla Verdi* (see page 76) or pork dishes, or it can be eaten by itself.

baby onions with balsamic sauce
cipolline al balsamico

These *cipolline* with their sweet and sour taste are delicious and can be served as part of an *antipasto* or to accompany hot and cold meat dishes.

SERVES 4

225 G (8 OZ) BABY ONIONS, PEELED
3 TABLESPOONS EXTRA VIRGIN OLIVE OIL
1 TABLESPOON BALSAMIC VINEGAR
2 TABLESPOONS RED WINE
SEA SALT

METHOD

Blanch the onions in plenty of boiling salted water for 15 minutes. Drain well. Sauté gently in the olive oil until golden brown. Add the vinegar, red wine and salt to taste, and cook briefly to allow the alcohol to evaporate.

courgettes with tomato and basil
zucchini al pomodoro e basilico

This extremely easy dish from Sicily makes a good accompaniment to fish and white meat. Choose small, firm courgettes.

SERVES 4

800 G (1¾ LB) COURGETTES
6 TABLESPOONS VIRGIN OLIVE OIL
2 GARLIC CLOVES, COARSELY CHOPPED
800 G (1¾ LB) RIPE TOMATOES, SKINNED, DESEEDED AND CHOPPED
1 BUNCH OF BASIL, CHOPPED
SALT

METHOD

Cut the courgettes into cubes and set aside. Heat the oil in a large pan, add the garlic and fry briefly. Stir in the tomatoes, basil and courgettes, then cover and cook gently for 15–18 minutes, until all the courgettes are tender. Season with salt and serve hot or cold.

broad beans and chicory
fave e cicorie ('ncapriata)

This is a peasant dish from Puglia, which I sampled in Lecce at a restaurant owned by Tonio Piceci – a gourmet who shares my passion for preserving regional food and features authentic local dishes on his menu. It is important to use the best-quality ingredients, such as really good olive oil and dried broad beans. In Puglia, the chicory used would be *catalogna puntarelle*, which is similar to dandelions. Wild dandelions can be substituted for the chicory in season, or you could use curly endive. This is eaten as a first course and is very filling.

SERVES 4

400 G (14 OZ) SKINLESS DRIED BROAD BEANS, SOAKED
  IN COLD WATER OVERNIGHT
1 POTATO, PEELED AND SLICED
1 CELERY STICK
1 RIPE TOMATO
1 SMALL ONION, PEELED
2 GARLIC CLOVES, PEELED
600 G (1 LB 5 OZ) CHICORY
SALT AND FRESHLY GROUND BLACK PEPPER
EXTRA VIRGIN OLIVE OIL, TO SERVE

METHOD

Drain the broad beans, put them in a pan and cover with fresh water. Add the potato, celery stick, tomato, onion and garlic cloves. Bring to the boil and simmer for 1 hour or until the beans are very tender. Discard the celery, tomato, onion and garlic – the potato will have disintegrated by now. Over a low heat, whisk the beans to a thick purée, adding a little hot water if necessary. Season to taste with salt and pepper and then set aside.

Cook the chicory in boiling salted water until just tender and then drain well. Serve the bean purée topped with the chicory and drizzled with abundant extra virgin olive oil.

charcoal-grilled wild mushrooms
funghi misti alla brace

If you are served grilled mushrooms in Italy they will usually be large porcini. However, during the mushroom season a variety of both wild and cultivated mushrooms may be used, resulting in an interesting mixture of textures, colours and flavours. This dish is a real delicacy, and ideal for vegetarians. In the South, and particularly in Puglia, the most popular mushroom is the *cardoncello*, a kind of very meaty oyster mushroom.

SERVES 4

800 G (1¾ LB) MIXED WILD MUSHROOMS (OR CULTIVATED ONES)

150 ML (5 FL OZ) EXTRA VIRGIN OLIVE OIL

JUICE OF ½ LEMON

3 TABLESPOONS VERY FINELY CHOPPED FRESH PARSLEY

1 CHILLI, VERY FINELY CHOPPED

1 GARLIC CLOVE, VERY FINELY CHOPPED

SALT AND FRESHLY GROUND BLACK PEPPER

METHOD

Thoroughly clean the mushrooms and cut any thick ones in half. Mix together the olive oil, lemon juice, parsley, chilli and garlic. Brush this mixture all over the mushrooms. Place the mushrooms on a charcoal grill and cook for just a few minutes if they are small, or longer for larger ones. Season with salt and pepper and serve immediately, either alone or as an accompaniment to grilled meat.

stuffed tomatoes
pomodori ripieni

One of the thousand ways of using tomatoes is as a container, enclosing some spicy ingredients. When cooked in the oven, the moisture in the tomato flesh concentrates the flavour of the stuffing. You end up with a dish which is sweet, provided you use ripe tomatoes, yet savoury. You can find this type of dish throughout the Mediterranean, stuffed with various fillings, including rice. I love it like this as a little snack or as part of an *antipasto*.

SERVES 4

4 x 200 G (7 OZ) LARGE RIPE BEEF TOMATOES

75 G (3 OZ) FRESH WHITE BREADCRUMBS

2 TABLESPOONS CHOPPED FRESH BASIL

2 TABLESPOONS CHOPPED FRESH MINT

½ GARLIC CLOVE, CRUSHED

SEA SALT

2 TABLESPOONS EXTRA VIRGIN OLIVE OIL

METHOD

Preheat the oven to 240°C/475°F/Gas Mark 9.

Cut the top off each tomato to form a lid and scoop out the seeds. Chop this central pulp and mix with the breadcrumbs, basil, mint, garlic and salt to taste. Refill the tomatoes and transfer to an ovenproof dish that will just hold them. Sprinkle with olive oil. Return the lids. Bake in the oven for 30 minutes.

red cabbage with apples

cavolo rosso con mele

Red cabbage, being spicy, goes well with all sorts of game, especially poultry such as goose and duck. I sometimes add some sweet apple juice instead of sugar, with wonderful results. I usually make more than necessary because it is so very good to eat and looks like a jam a couple of days later.

SERVES 4

1 SMALL ONION, FINELY CHOPPED

3 WHOLE DRIED CLOVES

2 TABLESPOONS EXTRA VIRGIN OLIVE OIL

500 G (1 LB 2 OZ) RED CABBAGE, FINELY SHREDDED

350 G (12 OZ) BRAMLEY APPLES, PEELED, CORED AND THINLY SLICED

375 ML (13 FL OZ) CHICKEN STOCK, OR A BOUILLON CUBE

10 G (¼ OZ) CASTER SUGAR

PINCH GROUND CINNAMON

SEA SALT

FRESHLY GROUND BLACK PEPPER

2 TEASPOONS WHITE WINE VINEGAR

METHOD

Fry the onion and cloves gently in the oil until soft but without colouring. Add the cabbage, apples, stock, sugar, cinnamon, salt and pepper. Simmer over a moderate heat for about 35 minutes until the apples have dissolved and the cabbage is tender, stirring from time to time to prevent sticking, and adding more water if necessary. Add the vinegar and simmer for a further 5 minutes.

baked potatoes calabrese-style
patate in tegame al forno

Although potatoes are widely used in Southern Italy, they are not a substitute for bread or pasta. Instead they are treated as a vegetable – served on their own or as an accompaniment to meat or fish. The best results for this recipe are obtained if you use a *tiano* (terracotta pot) and cook the potatoes in a wood-fired oven. But who today possesses such a 'luxury'? A deep baking dish and a conventional oven will do.

SERVES 6

1.5 KG (3¼ LB) POTATOES, PEELED AND SLICED, BUT NOT TOO THINLY

600 G (1 LB 5 OZ) LARGE, MEATY, RIPE TOMATOES, SLICED

20 FRESH BASIL LEAVES

120 G (4½ OZ) FRESH (*DOLCE*) PECORINO CHEESE, GRATED

50 G (2 OZ) DRIED BREADCRUMBS

120 ML (4 FL OZ) EXTRA VIRGIN OLIVE OIL

SALT AND FRESHLY GROUND BLACK PEPPER

METHOD

Preheat the oven to 200°C/400°F/Gas Mark 6.

In an ovenproof dish (preferably terracotta) build layers of potato, tomato and basil, sprinkling salt and pepper and grated pecorino cheese over each layer. Sprinkle the breadcrumbs over the top and pour over the olive oil. Add a little water and then bake for about 40 minutes, until the potatoes are tender.

rustic pugliese bread
pane casereccio

Nothing is thrown away in an Italian kitchen. Housewives often create works of art with leftovers! *Pane Casereccio* is made using all sorts of leftovers of cheese and meat which are still good to eat but too tough to slice. You can use any type of hard cheese, from grated Parmesan to pecorino, provolone or scamorza. Oddments of salami, ham or sausages can also be included.

MAKES 1 LARGE LOAF

25 G (1 OZ) FRESH YEAST OR 15 G (½ OZ) DRIED YEAST

175 ML (6 FL OZ) LUKEWARM WATER

2 TEASPOONS SALT

1 TEASPOON COARSELY GROUND BLACK PEPPER

3 TABLESPOONS VIRGIN OLIVE OIL

2 EGGS, BEATEN

600 G (1 LB 5 OZ) *DOPPIO ZERO* (00) FLOUR

150 G (5 OZ) LEFTOVER SALAMI, CUT INTO SMALL CUBES

150 G (5 OZ) LEFTOVER CHEESE, CUT INTO SMALL CUBES

2 TABLESPOONS DRIED BREADCRUMBS

METHOD

Dissolve the yeast in the water in a small bowl, then stir in the salt, pepper, oil and beaten eggs. Put the flour into a large bowl, make a well in the centre and pour in the yeast mixture. Mix well to make a dough. Knead for at least 20 minutes, until smooth and elastic. Sprinkle over the salami and cheese and gently knead them into the dough. With your hands, shape the dough into a longish sausage, then join both ends together to make a ring. Carefully transfer this to a baking tray dusted with the breadcrumbs. Cover and leave in a warm, draught-free place for 20 minutes, until slightly risen.

Preheat the oven to 200°C/400°F/Gas Mark 6.

Bake the loaf for 35 minutes, until it is golden brown on top and sounds hollow when tapped underneath.

focaccia

In my restaurant and also in our Carluccio's shop next door, we sell home-made focaccia. It is made with the best ingredients and everyone loves it! This flat bread can be served with many kinds of food, and is irresistible just out of the oven, cut in two like a sandwich with a slice of *mortadella* in the middle. Different varieties come topped with tomato, onions or herbs.

SERVES 4

FOR THE DOUGH

500 G (1 LB 2 OZ) STRONG WHITE PLAIN FLOUR

15 G (½ OZ) FRESH YEAST, OR DRY EQUIVALENT

300 ML (½ PINT) LUKEWARM WATER

2 TABLESPOONS EXTRA VIRGIN OLIVE OIL

10 G (¼ OZ) SEA SALT

FOR THE TOPPING

5 TABLESPOONS EXTRA VIRGIN OLIVE OIL

COARSE SEA SALT

FRESHLY GROUND BLACK PEPPER

(OR CHOPPED ONIONS, ROSEMARY OR OTHER HERBS)

METHOD

Preheat the oven to 240°C/475°F/Gas Mark 9.

Sift the flour into a bowl. Dissolve the yeast in the water and pour into a well in the middle of the flour, along with the oil and salt. Mix until a dough is formed and knead for about 10 minutes, until springy to the touch. Alternatively, mix all the ingredients in a food processor and, using the dough accessory, knead the bread for 2 minutes. Put into a bowl, cover with a damp tea towel and leave to prove for about 1 hour until it has doubled in size.

Knead the bread again to knock out any air bubbles and flatten out to an oval shape with your hands until 2.5 cm (1 in) thick. With the knuckles of your fingers press into the surface of the dough at 2.5 cm (1 in) intervals. Sprinkle with half the olive oil, then spread it gently over the surface with your finger tips. Sprinkle with salt and pepper or onions and herbs. Leave to rise again for about 30 minutes. Bake in the very hot oven for about 15 minutes until the base sounds hollow when tapped. Remove from the oven and sprinkle with the remaining oil.

salad of oranges and lemons
insalata di arance e limoni

For maximum flavour, this refreshing salad should be made with ripe, perfumed fruit. I was lucky enough to be able to pick fruit straight from the tree in an orange and lemon grove in Calabria. Southern Italian lemons are not as sour as ordinary ones. Unfortunately, they are difficult to find outside Italy but you could use grapefruit instead.

SERVES 4

4 ORANGES, PREFERABLY BLOOD ORANGES

4 LEMONS (NOT TOO SOUR) OR 2 GRAPEFRUIT

JUICE OF 1 LIME

4 TABLESPOONS EXTRA VIRGIN OLIVE OIL

SALT AND FRESHLY GROUND BLACK PEPPER

SPRIGS OF MINT, TO GARNISH

METHOD

Peel the oranges, removing all the white pith. Hold each orange in your hand and, with a small, sharp knife, cut out each segment from between the membranes. Peel the lemons or grapefruit, removing all the pith, and slice them thinly.

Put the fruit in a ceramic bowl. Whisk together the lime juice, olive oil and some salt and pour this dressing over the fruit. Grind over some black pepper, garnish with mint sprigs and serve. Excellent with cold meat or roasts.

peasant-style beans

fagioli alla cafona

I have finally found an Italian equivalent to beans on toast, but more interesting. *Cafone* is a derogatory word for peasant, and I must say if they came up with a recipe like this they must have been gourmet peasants. This dish is typical of the province of Caserta in Campania.

SERVES 4

300 G (11 OZ) FRESH CANNELLINI BEANS (OR USE 200 G/7 OZ
   DRIED BEANS, SOAKED OVERNIGHT, THEN DRAINED)
2 RIPE TOMATOES, DICED
1 CELERY STICK, FINELY CHOPPED
1 GARLIC CLOVE, FINELY CHOPPED
½ TEASPOON DRIED OREGANO
½ CHILLI, FINELY CHOPPED
6 TABLESPOONS EXTRA VIRGIN OLIVE OIL
4 LARGE SLICES OF TOASTED COUNTRY BREAD
SALT

METHOD

Put the cannellini beans in a large pan with enough water to cover, then bring to the boil and simmer for 1 hour or until just tender. Add the tomatoes, celery, garlic, oregano, chilli and oil and cook for 40 minutes or until the beans are soft. Add salt to taste and serve the soupy mixture on a slice of toasted bread in individual bowls. Drizzle some extra olive oil over, if desired.

6 desserts

orvieto aniseed biscuits anicini di orvieto ■ **pears in vin santo** pere al vin santo ■ **doges' delight ice-cream** la delizia dei dogi ■ **baked figs** fichi vanigliati al forno ■ **sicilian pastries** cannoli alla siciliana ■ **neapolitan struffoli** struffoli di napoli ■ **special lemon sorbet** sgroppino ■ **capri almond and chocolate cake** torta caprese di mandorle ■ **alessandro's tiramisù** tiramisù di alessandro ■ **fried peaches** pesche fritte ■ **pear zabaglione** zabaglione alla pera ■ **fried raviolo with orange-blossom honey** raviolo fritto al miele di fior d'arancio

orvieto aniseed biscuits
anicini di orvieto

I wanted to recreate this recipe after having seen and tasted these biscuits in a very fine delicatessen in Orvieto. They are good dipped in a dessert wine, as they do locally, or simply eaten as a biscuit. Since they are made with olive oil instead of butter, they are suitable for people who cannot eat dairy products.

MAKES APPROXIMATELY 20 BISCUITS

100 ML (3½ FL OZ) OLIVE OIL

100 ML (3½ FL OZ) WHITE WINE, PREFERABLY SWEET

75 G (3 OZ) CASTER SUGAR

150 G (5 OZ) PLAIN WHITE FLOUR

½ TEASPOON BICARBONATE OF SODA

2 TEASPOONS ANISE

1 TEASPOON FENNEL SEEDS

METHOD

Preheat the oven to 150°C/300°F/Gas Mark 2. Line a baking tray with greaseproof paper.

Put the oil, wine and sugar in a bowl and mix thoroughly. Then fold in the flour, bicarbonate of soda and spices.

Place teaspoons of the mixture onto the baking tray, spacing them well apart as they will spread during baking. Place in the oven and bake for 13 minutes or until golden brown.

Leave to cool on a wire rack so they become hard.

pears in vin santo
pere al vin santo

As a rule, in Italy dessert means fresh fruit. During the summer you are likely to get a basket of whatever is in season: cherries in June, apricots and plums in July, peaches and pears in August and then grapes. But in winter, baked or poached fruit like pears is very welcome. I find that the standard compote of apples mixed with other fruit can be boring, so here I have poached pears in Vin Santo and spices to create something truly wonderful.

SERVES 4

4 COMICE PEARS

1 x 750 ML BOTTLE VIN SANTO

100 G (4 OZ) CASTER SUGAR

RIND OF 1 LEMON

3 CLOVES

1 STICK OF CINNAMON

METHOD

First, peel the pears so that they can absorb the taste and golden colour of the wine, but leave them whole. Put them in a stainless steel saucepan just large enough to hold them and cover with the wine. Add the sugar, lemon rind and spices and poach for 40 minutes with the lid on. Remove the lid and cook for a further 10 minutes. Remove the pears from the liquid and set on one side. Boil the remaining liquid fast to reduce it to a thicker consistency. Pour this sauce over the pears, allow to cool and chill.

doges' delight ice-cream
la delizia dei dogi

I invented this recipe during a New Year's holiday in Venice in honour of the Doges, who were very much involved in bringing back from their expeditions in the Mediterranean all sorts of spices previously unknown in Italy. It uses saffron, the most precious of all spices, cardamom and cinnamon to make three ice-creams whose flavours blend marvellously well together.

MAKES 6 SERVINGS OF EACH FLAVOUR

FOR THE CINNAMON

500 ML (17 FL OZ) FULL-FAT MILK

2 TABLESPOONS GROUND CINNAMON

2 CLOVES

6 EGG YOLKS

50 G (2 OZ) HONEY (OPTIONAL)

150 G (5 OZ) CASTER SUGAR

150 ML (5 FL OZ) DOUBLE CREAM

FOR THE CARDAMOM

500 ML (17 FL OZ) FULL-FAT MILK

1 TABLESPOON CARDAMOM SEEDS, CRUSHED

6 EGG YOLKS

50 G (2 OZ) HONEY (OPTIONAL)

150 G (5 OZ) SUGAR

150 ML (5 FL OZ) DOUBLE CREAM

100 G (4 OZ) PISTACHIO NUTS

GREEN FOOD COLOURING

FOR THE SAFFRON

500 ML (17 FL OZ) FULL-FAT MILK

PINCH OF SAFFRON

6 EGG YOLKS

50 G (2 OZ) HONEY (OPTIONAL)

100 G (4 OZ) SUGAR

150 ML (5 FL OZ) DOUBLE CREAM

METHOD

The method is similar for each ice-cream flavour. In separate saucepans, bring to the boil the milk, cinnamon and cloves, milk and cardamom seeds, and milk and saffron. Simmer for 5–10 minutes. Allow to cool and strain.

In separate bowls mix the eggs, honey (if using) and the required quantity of sugar until creamy. To each bowl add the relevant flavoured milk a little at a time and whisk until it is all used up. Place the mixture back in the appropriate pans and cook in a bain-marie (a bowl over simmering hot water) for 15 minutes or until the mixture coats the back of a spoon. In order to avoid lumps, keep stirring. Leave for one or two days in the fridge. If you don't or can't, the texture and flavour of the finished result will not be as good, but you can cheat and put in a blender.

Then churn (in an ice-cream machine) for about 30 minutes. Add the semi-whipped cream (plus peeled, chopped pistachios and green colouring for the cardamom flavour) in the last 5 minutes, continue to churn and freeze.

Serve all three flavours together.

baked figs
fichi vanigliati al forno

Figs are eaten in all sorts of ways in Italy – fresh, dried, baked, etc. – but this simple recipe is particularly good. You could serve it with double cream. Italians, as a rule, don't, but the choice is yours.

SERVES 4

12 LARGE, RIPE FIGS

12 TABLESPOONS VANILLA SUGAR (OR USE CASTER SUGAR AND
A FEW DROPS OF VANILLA EXTRACT)

METHOD

Preheat the oven to 180°C/350°F/Gas Mark 4.

Carefully peel the figs and arrange them close together on a baking tray. Sprinkle a spoonful of vanilla sugar over each one. Bake for 5 minutes and then place under a hot grill for 2–3 minutes. The figs will exude a lovely pinkish syrup and their tops should be covered with a crust of sugar. They can be served hot but are also wonderful eaten chilled.

sicilian pastries

cannoli alla siciliana

There's a little work to do if you want to eat one of the best Southern specialities. Every bar or *pasticceria* in the South makes these pastries, which were originally the symbol of Sicily. They are eaten at any time as a pleasant little calorie shot to regenerate the powers! To shape the *cannoli* you will need some pieces of bamboo cane or metal tube, about 15 cm (6 in) long and 2 cm (¾ in) thick.

MAKES 16

25 G (1 OZ) BUTTER

25 G (1 OZ) CASTER SUGAR

1 EGG

3½ TABLESPOONS DRY WHITE WINE

2 TABLESPOONS VANILLA SUGAR

A PINCH OF SALT

150 G (5 OZ) *DOPPIO ZERO* (00) FLOUR

BEATEN EGG FOR SEALING THE CANNOLI

LARD OR VEGETABLE OIL FOR DEEP FRYING

ICING SUGAR FOR DUSTING

FOR THE FILLING

500 G (1 LB 2 OZ) VERY FRESH RICOTTA CHEESE

100 G (4 OZ) CASTER SUGAR

1 TABLESPOON VANILLA SUGAR

2 TABLESPOONS ORANGE FLOWER WATER

50 G (2 OZ) MIXED CANDIED PEEL, FINELY CHOPPED

50 G (2 OZ) CANDIED ANGELICA, FINELY CHOPPED

50 G (2 OZ) GLACÉ CHERRIES, FINELY CHOPPED

90 G (3½ OZ) PLAIN CHOCOLATE, FINELY CHOPPED

METHOD

To make the pastry, beat the butter and caster sugar together until light and creamy. Beat in the egg and then beat in the wine, vanilla sugar and salt. Mix in the flour and knead for 5–10 minutes, until smooth and elastic. Cover and leave in the fridge for at least 2 hours.

Roll out the dough until it is 2 mm (½ in) thick, then cut it into sixteen 12.5 cm (5 in) squares. Place a piece of bamboo cane or metal tube diagonally across each square of pastry and wrap 2 opposite corners around the cane. Seal with beaten egg. Make 3 or 4 at a time (this number will probably be dictated by the number of *cannoli* moulds you have).

Heat some lard or vegetable oil in a large deep pan – the fat must be deep enough to cover the *cannoli* completely. When it is very hot, carefully put in 3 or 4 *cannoli* and fry until golden brown – this will only take 1½–2 minutes. I find a long-pronged fork is the best implement for handling the *cannoli* in the boiling fat. Place the *cannoli* on kitchen paper to drain. When they are completely cool, remove the moulds.

To make the filling, beat the ricotta cheese with a fork, then mix in the caster sugar, vanilla sugar and orange flower water. The ricotta should become creamier in consistency. Stir in the candied peel, angelica, glacé cherries and chocolate. Fill the *cannoli* with the ricotta mixture and arrange on a plate. Dust with icing sugar and serve cool, but do not refrigerate.

neapolitan struffoli
struffoli di napoli

The origin of this classic recipe is the fruit of the imagination of the once poor people of Naples who make this dessert with fried pastry pellets substituting the more expensive hazelnuts. The recipe has a touch of Arabic influence to it due to frying in oil and flavouring with honey.

SERVES 10

5 MEDIUM EGGS

3 TABLESPOONS GRANULATED SUGAR

500 G (1 LB 2 OZ) *DOPPIO ZERO* (00) FLOUR

GRATED RIND OF 1 ORANGE

GRATED RIND OF 1 LEMON

1 TABLESPOON PURE ALCOHOL (IF NOT AVAILABLE, USE STRONG VODKA)

A PINCH OF SALT

OLIVE OIL OR LARD FOR DEEP FRYING

FOR THE CARAMEL

250 G (9 OZ) HONEY

100 G (4 OZ) CASTER SUGAR

2 TABLESPOONS WATER

FOR DECORATION

25 G (1 OZ) SMALL SUGAR SILVER BALLS

50 G (2 OZ) *CEDRO* (SEE BELOW), CUT INTO SMALL CUBES

RIND OF 1 TANGERINE, CUT INTO VERY THIN STRIPS

METHOD

To make the dough, beat the eggs lightly with the sugar, then mix in the flour, orange and lemon zest, alcohol and salt. Knead well for 3–4 minutes, then shape into a ball. Cover and leave to rest for 2 hours in a cool place.

Take a little bit of dough at a time and roll with your hand into sausage shapes about 1 cm (½ in) thick. Cut into pieces 1 cm (½ in) long. It is quite laborious rolling out the dough and will take you some time.

Heat the oil or lard in a pan so that it is 2.5 cm (1 in) deep. Fry the *struffoli*, quite a few at a time, in the hot oil until lightly browned, then remove and drain on kitchen paper.

To make the caramel, gently heat the honey, sugar and water in a large pan until the sugar has dissolved. Add the *struffoli* and stir carefully until they are all coated with the caramel. Arrange on a plate. Decorate with silver balls (not too many), *cedro* – a type of peel candied with sugar and green colouring to give it an exotic flavour – and tangerine rind, then leave to cool. They will taste delicious!

special lemon sorbet
sgroppino

Here is a suggestion for a dish that makes a perfect end to a meal or a break during a multi-course dinner. At La Taverna restaurant in Palau, Sardinia, we finished our excellent fish meal with this sorbet when we were filming there.

SERVES 4

6 SCOOPS OF LEMON ICE CREAM

100 ML (3½ FL OZ) ICED VODKA

2 GLASSES OF GOOD PROSECCO OR CHAMPAGNE

METHOD

For the best results you should use a blender and make sure all the ingredients are very cold, including the glasses in which they are to be served. Put all the ingredients into the blender and blend until you get a firm and frothy consistency. Serve immediately in glasses, with spoons.

capri almond and chocolate cake
torta caprese di mandorle

Amongst all the magnificent Southern cakes and tarts, the *Torta Caprese* is notable for the splendid result that is obtained with relatively little effort. 'A piece of cake,' you might say.

MAKES A 25 CM (10 IN) CAKE

200 G (7 OZ) BITTER CHOCOLATE

200 G (7 OZ) BUTTER, SOFTENED

6 EGGS, SEPARATED

200 G (7 OZ) CASTER SUGAR

50 G (2 OZ) *DOPPIO ZERO* (00) FLOUR

½ TEASPOON BAKING POWDER

300 G (11 OZ) BLANCHED ALMONDS, FINELY CHOPPED

2 TABLESPOONS STREGA LIQUEUR

ICING SUGAR FOR DUSTING

METHOD

Preheat the oven to 180°C/350°F/Gas Mark 4.

Break up the chocolate, put it in a pan with the butter and melt over a low heat. Leave to cool.

Beat the egg yolks with the sugar until thick and pale, then fold in the flour and baking powder. Carefully fold in the chocolate mixture, almonds and Strega. In a separate bowl, beat the egg whites until stiff and then gently fold them into the mixture. Pour into a buttered shallow 25 cm (10 in) cake tin and bake for 30 minutes, until well risen. If you test it with a skewer, the cake should still be a little moist in the centre. Turn out on to a wire rack and leave to cool, then dust with icing sugar.

alessandro's tiramisù
tiramisù di alessandro

I was brought up in a family where good food is very important – the preparation as well as the eating. So when I was in Italy recently I was glad to see that one of my nephews, Alessandro, has inherited the family's culinary enthusiasm. I watched him making tiramisù, a popular dessert with various versions in Italy. This is one of the simplest, but the most traditional. Because this recipes includes raw eggs, it should be consumed immediately.

SERVES 4

2 EGGS

2 TABLESPOONS CASTER SUGAR

FEW DROPS OF VANILLA ESSENCE

250 G (9 OZ) MASCARPONE

MILK, IF NECESSARY

20 SAVOIARDI BISCUITS

180 ML (6 FL OZ) STRONG BLACK ESPRESSO COFFEE

4 TABLESPOONS MARSALA

½ TABLESPOON COCOA POWDER

METHOD

Separate the eggs and beat the yolks with the sugar and vanilla essence. Add the Mascarpone and mix well to a creamy consistency, adding a little milk if the mixture is too thick. In another bowl beat the eggs whites until stiff, then fold them into the Mascarpone mixture.

Mix the coffee and Marsala in a bowl and dip in each biscuit for a second or two, making sure they do not break. Line the bases of four bowls with the biscuits, top with the Mascarpone mixture and chill for an hour. Dust with cocoa powder and serve.

fried peaches
pesche fritte

This recipe is my invention, using Southen ingredients in a Northern way. The result is delicious, I'm sure you'll agree.

SERVES 8

250 G (9 OZ) CASTER SUGAR

300 G (11 OZ) RICOTTA CHEESE

½ TEASPOON CINNAMON

3 HARD-BOILED EGG YOLKS

8 RIPE PEACHES

FLOUR, FOR DUSTING

1 EGG, BEATEN

DRIED BREADCRUMBS FOR COATING

OLIVE OIL, FOR DEEP FRYING

METHOD

Put the sugar, ricotta, cinnamon and hard-boiled egg yolks in a bowl and mix together well, then pass through a sieve. (Alternatively, you can whizz everything together in a food processor.) Chill for 2 hours, until firm.

Cut the peaches in half, then twist and remove the stone carefully with a sharp knife. Take a small scoop and remove a little of the flesh from the centre. Mix the scooped-out flesh with the ricotta mixture and then fill the peach halves with this. Dust the peaches in flour, then coat with beaten egg and finally coat with dried breadcrumbs.

Heat the olive oil and deep fry the peaches for a few seconds, until golden brown. They can be served hot or cold.

pear zabaglione
zabaglione alla pera

Experimenting with zabaglione, I discovered that a great variety of flavours could be achieved by substituting different liquids for the traditional Marsala. I had the most success with Poire William liqueur but Cointreau and blackberry and raspberry liqueurs also worked well. Using the egg yolks as a vehicle for the flavouring, it's up to you to discover new combinations – perhaps even trying fresh fruit juices such as passion fruit.

SERVES 4

12 FREE RANGE EGG YOLKS

4 TABLESPOONS CASTER SUGAR

120 ML (4 FL OZ) POIRE WILLIAM LIQUEUR

METHOD

Put the egg yolks and sugar in a large bowl, preferably a copper one, and whisk until thick and pale. Add the liqueur and mix well. Set the bowl over a pan of barely simmering water, making sure the water is not touching the base of the bowl, and whisk constantly until the mixture becomes a thick foam. Pour into glasses and serve immediately, accompanied by little biscuits such as amarétti, if desired.

fried raviolo with orange-blossom honey

raviolo fritto al miele di fior d'arancio

To do justice to the exceptionally good orange-blossom honey from Pietro Pizzimenti in Calabria, I borrowed a recipe from Sardinia because I thought the two would combine to produce perfection. The Sardinian raviolo called *sabadas*, or *sebadas*, is usually flavoured with local honey but I find the Calabrese honey quite irresistible.

SERVES 4

4 PIECES OF PECORINO CHEESE, CUT INTO CIRCLES 10 CM (4 IN)
   IN DIAMETER AND 5 MM (¼ IN) THICK
OLIVE OIL FOR DEEP FRYING
120 ML (4 FL OZ) ORANGE-BLOSSOM HONEY

FOR THE DOUGH
150 G (5 OZ) *DOPPIO ZERO* (00) FLOUR
1 EGG
1 EGG YOLK
A PINCH OF SALT
1 TABLESPOON CASTER SUGAR

METHOD

To make the dough, pile the flour up into a volcano shape on a work surface and make a large well in the centre. Put the egg, egg yolk, salt and sugar in the well and beat lightly with a fork. With your hands, gradually mix in the flour. When the mixture has formed a dough, knead it well with the palms of your hands for about 10 minutes, until it is very smooth and elastic. Cover and leave to rest for 20 minutes.

Roll out the dough until it is about 3 mm (⅛ in) thick. Cut out 8 rounds 15 cm (6 in) in diameter, re-rolling the trimmings as necessary. Put a piece of pecorino cheese in the centre of 4 of the rounds. Brush the edges of the dough rounds with water and cover with the remaining dough rounds, gently pressing the edges together to seal.

Heat plenty of olive oil in a pan and fry the ravioli for about 3–4 minutes, until brown and crisp on both sides. Put on individual serving plates, pour the honey over and serve immediately.

index